Dale J.

W9-DFK-977

SERMON STORIES
OF
FAITH AND HOPE

SERMON STORIES
of
FAITH and HOPE

By

WILLIAM L. STIDGER

UNITY SCHOOL LIBRARY
Unity Village
Lee's Su......., ... 64063

WITHDRAWN
by Unity Library

ABINGDON PRESS
New York • *Nashville*

SERMON STORIES OF FAITH AND HOPE

Copyright MCMXLVIII by Stone & Pierce

All rights in this book are reserved.
No part of the book may be used or reproduced in
any manner whatsoever without written permission of
the publishers except brief quotations embodied in
critical articles or reviews. For information address
Abingdon Press, Nashville 2, Tennessee.

Library of Congress Catalog Card Number: 48-1905

D

SET UP, PRINTED, AND BOUND BY THE
PARTHENON PRESS, AT NASHVILLE,
TENNESSEE, UNITED STATES OF AMERICA

BV
4225
·S685

Dedicated to
DR. WALTER MUELDER
A DYNAMIC DEAN
A FAITHFUL FRIEND AND
AS THE THEOLOGICAL STUDENTS SAY
"A GREAT GUY!"

CONTENTS

THE HOW AND WHY OF THIS BOOK

THIS book of sermon stories grows out of a year's writing of a syndicated newspaper column which I have run for eight years. I cull from that column "Berries for the King's Plate." I get the stories from preachers, students, friends; from a wide reading in ancient and modern literature; and from a varied contact with the great and the humble of the earth whom I interview for magazine writing. Stories flock to me like steel filings to a magnet because people know that I like to get them.

WILLIAM L. STIDGER

"TEARS AT MY FINGER TIPS"

ONE of my students once told me a story which made me more thoughtful of other people and their troubles.

In his college dining room there was a popular Negro woman who waited on the table. We'll call her "Mary." All the students liked her, for she always had a big smile, did her work so buoyantly and happily, had gay repartee with the boys, and yet was never fresh. She gave as much as she received and never more in comebacks. Those bright young college boys found Mary quick on the trigger and they never got ahead of her.

On this particular morning, in the rush of the usual late breakfast just before the eight o'clock class, when the students were all rushing in at the last minute to grab a bite and beat the bell, suddenly there was a crash. Mary had dropped a whole platter of dishes with an unearthly bang. She stooped over, greatly embarrassed, to pick up that tray-load of dishes and wipe the scrambled eggs and coffee stains from the floor.

At this, loud guffaws, a chorus of wisecracks, and plenty of laughter focused on Mary, their old-time friend and comrade. That was their opportunity to kid Mary and they did not muff it. In fact, a perfect avalanche of laughter and a bombardment of gay remarks crashed down upon the embarrassed Mary.

When Mary had picked up the wreckage and wiped the floor, she waited until the boys had expended all their ammunition of kidding, and then said quietly to them: "Boys, I guess I'ze jest got tears at my finger tips, for my boy was killed in Italy yesterday, and I just got word. I thinks I'ze jest got tears at my finger tips, I has!"

A silence fell over that dining room, and a lot of boys had embarrassed looks on their faces. That simple statement struck them like a ton of bricks and they were all apology and penitence. But it taught them a lesson. It taught them that often when people stumble and fall, when they don't seem to be able to co-ordinate enough to do their work, when their eyes will not focus, their fingers are clumsy, their physical responses sluggish, it may be that they have tears at their finger tips.

❖❖❖

"A TENDER CARE THAT NOTHING BE LOST"

ONE of my boys was captain of a transport during the war and he told me of a dramatic incident which happened on one of his trips across the storm-tossed Atlantic. Early one morning the ships of that convoy received an emergency order to stop and maneuver into a circle surrounding a small destroyer. It was a strange order in mid-Atlantic and everyone was puzzled over it. But it was an order and it was immediately obeyed.

Two days later they were informed that on that small destroyer there was a boy who was seriously in need of an operation, but the destroyer was tossing about so much it was impossible to operate unless the ship could lie in a comparatively calm area. Those large ships were turned from their courses and their progress was slowed to form a protective breakwater for the small ship so that the emergency operation could be performed to save the lad's life. Unusual? Yes. But in exactly the spirit of one of Galileo's famous sayings. That great scientist once said: "I have noticed that the sun which holds the whirling stars, planets, and worlds in place in the universe, also has time to ripen a bunch of grapes on the vines of Italy." To me that is one of the most profound statements I have ever read.

It is also in the mood of one of the best-known statements in the Bible: that God is so all-loving, so tender and thoughtful that the hairs of a man's head are numbered and that God makes note even of the falling of a sparrow. I am glad that the translators used the humble, lowly sparrow in that figure of speech, for all over this earth the most common bird we know is the sparrow. So it was that we are taught that nothing is too common, no human being too poor or too insignificant to be in the loving care and keeping of the heavenly Father and of the universal laws which he instigated and controls. It is a heartening, a helpful, and a hopeful thought that the admiral of an Atlantic fleet crossing the seas in wartime would stop a convoy to save the life of a boy, and that the same sun which holds the worlds in their orbits also has time to ripen a bunch of grapes.

An even more dramatic and climactic statement of this loving care of the heavenly Father for an individual comes from Dr. Alfred North Whitehead, of Harvard: "The image under which the nature of God can best be conceived is that of a tender care that nothing be lost." That understanding statement comes from Dr. Whitehead's book *Process and Reality,* and was pointed out to me by John Laveley, one of my students.

❖❖❖

"I KEEP MY EYES ON THE SUNRISE"

A FRIEND of mine, John Crummey, president of Food Machinery, uses the airplane for transcontinental trips just as some business men use trains to commute between New York and suburban towns each day. He has had many fascinating experiences on planes.

One day he was coming east from San Francisco and it was a rough trip. Nearly every passenger was sick. A fine-looking, mature, gray-haired woman got on the plane at Kansas City, heard the passengers tell about how sick they had been for hours, and what a very rough trip it had been. She smiled. They tried to tell her that she would also be ill before long because it was still stormy and bumpy in the air. Still she smiled kindly and confidently as if to assure them that she would *not* be sick.

The plane rose gracefully from the airport just as the sun was coming up out of the long, low, level land of Missouri. She sat in her seat completely absorbed in the beauty of that sunrise—and what a glorious thing a sunrise can be ten thousand feet in the air as it comes up above the plains or behind hills and bursts through the clouds! There is no more beautiful sight on earth. That sun illuminates great mountain-like ranges of white, gray, and black clouds until it looks as if some master like Turner is painting a gorgeous sky-canvas in your very presence.

The eastbound plane had hardly reached its flying level until it began to drop five hundred feet at a clip into a deep well of loneliness, like an elevator dropping suddenly from the top of the Empire State Building to the bottom. There was a sinking sensation in the pit of each passenger's stomach, sweat broke out on most of their foreheads, accompanied by an uneasy upheaval of their interiors, and, once again they were all on the way to abject sickness. However, the gray-haired woman sat calmly, benignly, and placidly undisturbed by the sensation of the upheaving and downdropping of that huge plane. My friend John Crummey, sitting beside that calm woman, said: "I'm surprised that you don't get airsick!"

She turned to him, smiled graciously, and said: "I have a preventative for air sickness this morning."

14

"For goodness sake, what is it?" asked Mr. Crummey. "Tell me so that I can try it."

She replied: "I keep my eyes on the sunrise."

❖❖❖

ARE YOU WORTH SAVING?

THE late Bishop Bruce Baxter knew how to follow in the footsteps of his Master, who taught his great truths through parables or short stories, and, because of that ability, he was what someone called "a person as well as a parson." He was also a fascinating preacher, and instead of emptying auditoriums, he filled them. People always went away from a Bishop Baxter sermon with something they could remember and apply to life, and he preached in a way that "a wayfaring man, though a fool, and a little child" never erred in understanding what he said. That is a high and holy art.

Once I heard him tell a story about a small boy who was playing on a pier at the summer resort where the boy's parents lived. Sandy suddenly fell into the water beyond his depth and yelled for help because he could not swim a stroke.

A man, walking along the shore, heard his distress calls, threw off his coat and plunged into the lake, got his strong arms around that struggling boy, swam to shore with him, and saved the boy's life. By that time the father and mother, having also heard the boy's cry for help, had come to the end of the pier, frantic with fear. There was a good deal of excitement in the whole camp, for most of the inhabitants had gathered in time to see the rescue and to help the exhausted man climb up on the dock with the limp figure.

They gave the boy artificial respiration, and had worked over him for ten minutes when suddenly the boy opened his eyes, came to consciousness, and saw his rescuer leaning over him solicitously. Into the face of the man who had saved his life the boy looked earnestly and said: "Thank you, sir, for saving my life!"

"That's all right, son, glad to do it. But see to it that you're worth saving!"

The man walked away through the crowd, and disappeared. Neither the parents nor the boy himself ever saw that man again. He was a stranger in that community and nobody knew who he was. It is unnecessary to add that the boy never forgot the experience—that day or that man —and all his life the admonition of that stranger rang in his heart and in his experience: "That's all right, son, glad to do it. But see to it that you're worth saving!" And Bishop Baxter did see to it that he was worth saving.

❖❖❖

"I AIN'T NO FOOL, MISTER!"

DR. JAMES McCONNELL, of Oklahoma City, told me a glorious story.

One day as he was fishing on the Missouri River on a day's outing, he suddenly saw a boy frantically waving a red flag from a temporary dock of homemade piling jutting out into the river. Dr. McConnell looked up and saw a large Missouri River steamboat coming down the water full steam ahead. It looked to him as if that barefooted farmer boy was trying to flag that swiftly moving boat. Moved by curiosity he pulled in his fish pole and walked to where the boy was waving the red flag. He began to talk with him.

"You don't mean to tell me that you are fool enough to think that great river boat will respond to your signal and try to stop at this little dock on the bend of a swift-moving river?"

"Sure I do, Mister. It'll stop all right. It'll stop."

16

"Why that boat couldn't stop on this bend in the river to come in here even if they paid any attention to your flag," said Dr. McConnell.

"They'll stop all right, Mister! They'll stop. I ain't afraid they won't stop!"

"You certainly are the biggest fool I ever saw to think that big boat would pay any attention to a boy's signal on this bend in the river and stop at this God-forsaken spot!"

Just at that moment, much to his surprise, Dr. McConnell saw the great river boat make a sudden swerve out of its downriver course, heard the whistle blow twice in recognition of the signal. Then the steamboat slowly made its way into the crude homemade dock on piles. The gangplank was run out, the boy stepped on board, looked over his shoulder at the stranger standing on the shore, and said: "I ain't no fool, Mister, my father's the captain of this boat!"

Need anything be added to the bare facts of that story to an imaginative group of readers such as I have? Nothing!

❖❖❖

"DIPPED IN SUNSHINE"

I WAS recently reading one of the best biographies ever written—*The Life of Alice Freeman Palmer,* written by her husband, the Harvard philosopher. Alice Freeman Palmer was the second president of Wellesley College.

In the biography Dr. Palmer tells of talking with a Wellesley girl about Mrs. Palmer and the impression that great spirit made on her students. The girl said: "When I was called into her office, either for commendation, a social visit, or for a reprimand, I left her office and her presence feeling as if I had been dipped in sunshine."

That, to me, is as beautiful an expression of what happens to a person when that person has been in the presence of

17

a kindly, loving soul, as any expression I have ever heard, and I set it down here because I got a real kick out of it, and because it points the way for each of us to get more out of life and to help others to get more out of life. It is a glorious thing to have such kindness in our hearts that when people come into our very presence they feel as if they had been dipped in sunshine. Jesus must have been such a person when he walked the ways of human life, and his contemporaries, such as the woman at the well of Jacob, the blind man, the woman who was sick with an issue of blood, the man at the well of bubbling waters in Jerusalem, the thief on the cross, the woman taken in adultery, must have felt as if they had been "dipped in sunshine."

I happen to know a few people like that in everyday life. One is a Negro janitor, named Saunders Wilkins, on Beacon Hill in Boston. Another is a nurse, Sadie Hagen, of The Deaconess Hospital in Boston. There are Marie Cole Powell, a teacher and writer in Concord, Massachusetts; Miss Mary Scott in Moundsville, West Virginia, a simple, unselfish, cultured woman in a small town who has literally devoted her life to others; and a woman who works in our home one day a week. Her name is Lucy and I like to be at home when she is there because she is so happy, so pleasant, so uniformly faithful to her tasks. Another is my grocer, a Jewish merchant named Block. When I come away from the presence of these everyday people I feel as if I had been "dipped in sunshine."

It is said that one day a confrere asked William E. Gladstone why it was that he was so uniformly happy, and he replied: "Because I have been living with a rose all my married life." Mrs. Gladstone evidently made that great English prime minister feel as if he had been "dipped in sunshine."

❖❖❖

THE MIRACLE OF A FATHER'S FAITH

EDDIE is an automobile salesman—and a good one. He is a man of no great education but of great character. He is also a fine father and has raised and educated five sons on a small income.

Several summers ago he put his ten-year-old son in a boy's camp. The older boys had gone off to war and that last son was precious to them.

One hot summer afternoon word came from the camp that the boy had been stricken with what they thought was infantile paralysis. The parents were frightened, and Eddie, the father, hurried to the camp near Boston. The boy lay motionless, for he could not move a muscle in his body.

"Hello, Sonny! How's the old boy?" the father said, greeting him as if nothing very serious had happened, although his own mind and heart were almost paralyzed with anxiety and terror.

The boy began to cry and said to him: "I don't feel so good, Dad, and besides, I'm the only boy in this whole camp that hasn't a camera!"

"Why didn't you tell me, Sonny? You'll have a camera before the sun sets tonight or I'm not your Dad!"

When Eddie came away from that paralyzed boy the doctor said to him: "It's a serious case. Two boys who were stricken are unconscious and we don't expect them to live. We won't know about your boy for forty-eight hours. We'll just have to wait."

Eddie went home, scoured the stores in Boston for a camera. They were hard to get that war year. He said to his wife: "That kid's going to have his camera no matter what it costs. We can't afford to get it, but we can't afford not to get it."

The boy got his camera. Eddie took it to the camp and

laid it down on his son's bed. The boy smiled, grabbed the camera, and in half an hour was sitting up in bed, his face shining, examining his new camera, the infantile paralysis having disappeared.

"The Doc said it was a miracle, for two other boys who were stricken in that camp died." Eddie said to me: "I also think it was a miracle from God, don't you?"

"No, Eddie, I think it was a miracle from a father—a father's faith and love."

"IF MY FATHER HOLDS THE ROPE?"

A SCIENTIST was searching for certain bird eggs and found a nest of what he wanted on the edge of a steep cliff overhanging the sea on the Atlantic coast. He asked a local boy to allow himself to be lowered down that cliff on a rope to get the eggs. The pay was high and the boy needed the money because he was going off to college the next September.

However, the danger terrified him. But finally, after much thought, and weighing the pros and cons, he suddenly said: "I'll do it providing my father holds the rope!"

This reminds me of a broadcast of the Quiz Kids one Sunday afternoon. Joe Kelley asked the kids who was their hero, and Gerald replied, with a little embarrassment, almost in stuttering words: "Well—a—hem—I guess—just—now—my—father—is—my hero!"

And that, in turn, sent me back a long distance to something Shakespeare said:

> To you your father should be as a god;
> One that composed your beauties, yea, and one
> To whom you are but as a form in wax
> By him imprinted and within his power
> To leave the figure or disfigure it.

One day I watched Joe Cronin's young son at a Red Sox ball game in Boston. Joe was pinch-hitting. He slashed a two-bagger directly over the second baseman's head and brought in two runs in the ninth inning which won the game. It was a daring thing for a manager to do, to put himself in to pinchhit in that crucial spot. The crowd went wild. After the noise of the crowd had died down that kid yelled so we could all hear him, yelled with a note of pride in which we all shared: "That's my Pop!" I think a good many of us fathers who heard that boy yell must have said in explanation of the tears in our eyes: "Its the wind!"

❖❖❖

ON HAVING A CENTER

REAR ADMIRAL RICHARD E. BYRD is a human sort of person, as well as an explorer and a philosopher. Several times I have interviewed him, written about him, and broadcast his dramatic story. One of my broadcasts caught him listening and shortly after it was over he called me on the telephone asking for a copy of the script, saying: "Whenever anybody says something good about me I like to send it to my mother." I loved him for that spirit.

Once he told me of a dangerous experience he had on his first expedition to the South Pole. He left his isolated hut for a brief exploration trip and got lost in a blizzard. Nothing about him gave him a sense of direction. If he should strike out blindly and fail in the first attempt to get back to his hut, he would be lost, and likely freeze to death.

I had a long pole which I always carried with me to feel for holes in the ice. I drove it into the snow and tied a scarf to its top, which blew in the terrific winds. That was my center. If I failed to find the hut, I could at least return to that pole.

Three times I struck out in search of my hut, each time failing to find it. However, each time I returned to my center, without which I would have been irrevocably lost, and perhaps have died. In the fourth attempt I accidentally stumbled upon my hut.

I always use that experience to say to people that it is a good thing to have a center—something to guide you, something you are certain about. It may be your Bible, it may be your religion, your wife, children, friends, your national ideals, your conscience—something to which you can return in the storms and uncertainties of life to get your bearings. It's a good thing to have some center in life.

❖❖❖

WE'VE STILL TO LEARN

A BOY who took part in the invasion of Italy was telling me a remarkable story recently that has significance for all of human life, especially for our personal and international relationships. If we should all take this story to heart we would certainly get a lot more out of life. The story gave me one of the biggest kicks I have ever got out of a story.

This American boy, just a simple, everyday lad, was billeted in an Italian home. The home was humble, even more so than his own American home; so crude and unfurnished that he had rather a quiet contempt for the family. There was only a bare table, no chairs, and certainly no table cloth on the table, although the house was immaculately clean.

One evening, sitting in the yard under the grapevines, the American boy and the Italian family were watching a crescent-shaped moon sailing majestically over Mount Vesuvius, from which was belching a tall column of smoke, and down whose rugged sides there was a flowing stream of molten red lava which could be easily seen in the darkness. The night was majestic and beautiful; the mood of the group was serious and silent. The futility of war and the inhumanity of man to man was the subject of conversation, although they did not use those lofty phrases. Suddenly the conversation and silence of that beautiful night was broken by the roar of fifty American planes from Foggia which swept over their heads on some mission of destruction. After the planes had droned off in the distance, the old father of the Italian family softly remarked: "We have learned to swim like the fish under the sea; we have learned to fly like the birds in the air, but we have not yet learned to walk the earth in peace with our fellow men."

When the boy told me of that simple and yet profound statement made by a supposedly ignorant Italian father in that humble home in which he was billeted, he said: "That observation certainly had a wallop in it, didn't it?"

"Yes, son, it certainly had a wallop in it—and still has. We hope that we are now, through our United Nations, on the way we learn to walk with our fellow men in brotherhood and peace, don't we?"

The boy answered fervently: "I'll say we do! It's about time!"

❖❖❖

"THE MASTER'S SPIRIT"

THE late Charles J. Connick, the master stained-glass craftsman, used to have showings of his great windows in his Boston studio before they were installed in cathedrals and churches. Following those studio showings he would have a dinner for a small group of intimate friends. I was fortunate to be in that group, and it was like a pentecostal experience to hear the talk that went around that table in the studio.

One day Mr. Connick was telling us about a young artist who was studying with a great master in the craft (we suspected that it was Connick), and one day the young artist came to the master and begged that he might have

23

the privilege of using some of the master's own tools with which he worked.

"What do you want my tools for, son?"

"Oh, I just want them to see if it will make any difference in the work I do," replied the apprentice.

A week later the master walked into the boy's presence and said: "Well, Son, how are you doing with my tools?"

"Not so good, master, not so good! In fact my work is not one whit better than it was, even working with your tools."

A gray-haired old artist, overhearing the conversation between the apprentice and the master, winked at the master and said to the young boy: "Son, it isn't the tools of the master that you need; it's the master's spirit."

And never was a truer word spoken than that! It reminds us all of a pertinent quotation from Romans (8:9): "Now if any man have not the Spirit of Christ, he is none of his."

❖❖❖

KEEP YOUR PARACHUTES
IN GOOD REPAIR

DURING World War II I spoke at one of our largest airfields, at Rantoul, Illinois, and during my stay there the Commandant courteously took me on an inspection tour and showed me everything that was not a strict military secret. The most interesting room he showed me was the room where hundreds of soldiers were inspecting parachutes.

I noticed the meticulous care with which they worked on those chutes, and asked permission to talk with some of the soldiers.

"You men seem to bestow great care on those chutes. You work just as if you were going to have to drop in one of them yourselves."

One soldier grinned and replied: "Sir, that is exactly what

24

we have to do. The rule around here is that each fellow who works on one of these chutes has to take the first jump in it. You're right! I'll say we give them careful attention. I suppose they have that rule so that we'll be very careful in our work on them. When you have to drop in the one you yourself inspect, you're careful in your inspection."

I came away from that room with the feeling that that was a very pragmatic rule. I came away from that room thinking in terms of human life, thinking of the parachutes of everyday life, over which we ought to work more meticulously than some of us do.

There is the parachute of education. Most young people have, at best, a casual attitude toward education, but if they ever stopped to think that in the future the parachute of education was to mean either life or death to them, either failure or success, my guess would be that they would build that educational parachute with infinite care and labor.

There is also the parachute of friendship. A famous author of long ago said that the most important thing in human happiness is "to keep your friendships in good repair." When I first heard that wise saying it did not make much impression on my adolescent mind, but as life has moved forward with rapid speed and I have noticed that every single promotion, every important position, every great move in my life, has come because of the recommendation or the importuning of some personal friend, I have come to realize that it is a good thing to keep all friendships in good repair.

Then there is the parachute of health. When Glenn Frank, on his fiftieth birthday, was asked to give advice to young college students, he said: "If I were twenty years of age again I would take such good care of my health that, when the years of great tasks and opportunities came to me in my forties, I would have a sound constitution to carry on those tasks." What he meant was that he would take such meticulous care in building, constructing, and inspecting the parachute of good health that when a crisis came, and he had to make a jump of ten thousand feet, his parachute of health would be in good condition to land him safely.

Lastly I think of the parachute of religious faith. Most of us are raised in Christian homes and the church. We go to Sunday school; we learn the great moral and spiritual principles of life. And many of us look upon that process as a bore, and treat it more or less casually and rebelliously. But as life moves along most of us come to learn that the parachute of faith is a good thing to "keep in repair."

❖❖❖

"WHEN DO I CROAK, DOC?"

JIMMY CHUBB, as we minister friends call him, one of our great rural preachers, told me the story of a young boy who was called upon to give his small brother a blood transfusion because of a serious accident in which he had a dangerous loss of blood.

The older brother was called to the hospital suddenly and was hurriedly prepared for the transfusion. His father had driven the boy to the hospital but, as is the way of even thoughtful parents, doctors and nurses in an emergency, had not explained what a transfusion meant.

The boy donned the hospital garb, and lay down beside his brother. The needle was inserted in the left arm, and he watched his pallid brother lying unconscious beside him. He looked up at the doctor who was making the transfusion, and said, as seriously as a young boy could say anything: "When do I croak, Doc?"

He knew nothing about transfusions, and as no one had explained to him that it was a harmless experience to a

26

healthy body, he had actually felt during all the hurried trip to the hospital and the transfusion itself that they were asking him to give his life for his younger brother. That one question, "When do I croak, Doc?" revealed to the doctor, nurses, and his parents that he had never raised a question about it. A dramatic moment!

The boy's mother wept when she heard that question, as did one of the nurses; the two men blinked their eyes, coughed, and the doctor asked the nurse for a towel to wipe something from his eye. But everyone in the room knew what made the physician blink, and what made me blink when Jimmy Chubb told me the story. And everyone of us will hear the echoing memory of a great Bible verse: "Greater love hath no man than this, that a man lay down his life for his friends."

❖❖❖

FRATERNIZATION DE LUXE

A YOUNG Methodist army officer told me this story of fraternization in Germany. He and a group of his men had just entered a small German village in the Ruhr. The German army had just fled, leaving destruction in its wake, and presumably many dangerous mines and booby traps. Orders were strict: there was to be positively no fraternization.

As these boys walked cautiously through the village they came to a small church, the doors of which were open. They walked in, watching every door, scanning the floor and pews for traps. My young friend naturally walked up to the organ for he had been a church organist at home in his little Texas town. A hymnbook was lying on the music rack, open at the page of the hymn "A Mighty Fortress Is Our God." He couldn't resist the temptation to sit down

27

and play that hymn. For three long years he hadn't touched the keys of an organ, much less played or seen one.

He opened the stops, and, as he told me: "I went to town on that mighty old hymn which has been the favorite of Germans and Americans for centuries." As he played he heard footsteps, or sensed that he did, for he looked over his shoulder and saw two very elderly persons, evidently a man and his wife, reverently walking down the center aisle to sit in the front pew. He smiled at them and continued playing *"Ein' Feste Burg."* Then came a young couple into the church, and before he finished playing the hymn he counted twenty people sitting reverently listening. They had not heard a religious service for many months and their hearts were as hungry as his to hear organ music. Before he was through, the Germans joined in and they all sang that great universal hymn together, American soldiers and German civilians. Before he got up from the organ seat he wondered what he should do as an American officer about those strict orders against fraternization. Should he speak to them or arrest them? He was frankly puzzled, but a crippled old German settled it. When the American left the organ the old man hobbled to him, tears running down his gray cheeks, threw his arms around him saying over and over: *"Mein Bruder! Mein Bruder!"* That settled the matter of fraternization in that young American officer's heart.

❖❖❖

"WATCHING GOD PUT THE WORLD TO BED"

A MOTHER I know called her five-year-old son to dinner five times. Like most boys of that age he did not come. He was busily engaged in some highly important activity, as small boys usually are when they are called to dinner, to wash their hands and neck, or told that it is time for bed.

Impatiently the mother said: "That's the fifth time I have called Billy to dinner and he doesn't come. I'll have to see about this. I'll spank that rascal and teach him to obey his mother and at least answer when I call him!"

Out she strode from the dining room toward the front porch, her skirts flying, an angry flush on her young face, and with malice, if not murder, in her heart.

"Young man, why don't you come to dinner when I call you? I've called you five times."

"But, mother, I only heard you call three times, and besides, I'm watching God put the world to bed."

Then for the first time the young mother looked up to where her young son pointed and saw a gorgeous, crimson, golden sunset, with deep dark clouds in the west fringed with silver and gold. It took her breath away. Tears ran down over her cheeks, and she grabbed the child, whom she was about ready to punish for not answering her, and said: "You darling, Billy, mother is glad to know that you are watching God put the world to bed and that is really more important than coming to dinner, isn't it?

"I'll say it is—and how!" replied her sophisticated five-year-old, with a grin of understanding, and then added another sentence which set little songs singing in that mother's heart: "It's a beautiful sunset, mother—a beautiful sunset, ain't it?"

"Billy, please don't say 'ain't,' but it is a beautiful sunset and God is putting the world to bed."

❖❖❖

"HE WALKS WHERE WE WALK"

DR. EUGENE ANTRIM, a minister in Oklahoma City, told me of an unusual experience he had a few years ago.

29

He was standing by a hotel window which faced a city street when he heard the squeal of streetcar brakes, then the cry of a hurt man. As he watched, he saw a large crowd gather around the streetcar which had stopped in front of the hotel.

Dr. Antrim hurried out to see what had happened. He saw a man under the streetcar suffering terribly. They tried to get him out but were unsuccessful. The police car came, and workmen from the streetcar line, but they soon saw that it would be necessary to send for heavy equipment from the carbarn to extricate him, and that would take a long time. The man was crying hysterically: "Get me out! Get me out of here—please!"

It was apparent that the shock of the accident, the pain, and the fear had made the man hysterical. What was to be done with him during the half hour or more that it would take to get machinery on the spot to lift that streetcar and release him?

A simple, ordinary, badly dressed bystander solved that problem. He came out of the crowd, crawled under the car, lay down beside the victim, put his arms around him, and began to talk kindly and softly into his ear. The man calmed down, stopped his frantic crying, his hysteria dissipated, his fears calmed, and he smiled into the stranger's face lying beside him and said: "Thank you, friend!"

In half an hour the lifting equipment came from the carbarns and they lifted the streetcar that pinned the man down. The ambulance took him away, and the man who lay down beside him quietly disappeared into the crowd, never to be found again.

Dr. Antrim says that the experience gave him more of a "kick" than he ever got out of a long and eventful life in the ministry, as it did me when he told me the story, for hidden in that kind act is the secret of universal happiness and international peace—the ability and willingness to walk where other people walk and to share their troubles, sufferings, and sorrows with them, both as individuals and as nations.

I once had a most successful student pastor in a labor community. His name was Dick Jones. I asked one of his laymen what accounted for this student's unusual success and that layman answered: "He walks where we walk!"

❖❖❖

A CONTAGIOUS DISEASE

AFTER World War II we were warned by the government of several diseases which our returning soldiers brought back from the South Sea Islands and the Pacific regions, as well as from European countries. Public precautions have been taken and scientific research has been thorough. The influenza epidemic following World War I is still remembered. It was terrible and completely swept the nation killing many people. We have, through scientific precautions, so far escaped that experience following World War II. This fact leads me naturally and smoothly toward the disease I want to tell about in this story. It is a disease which certainly helps us to get the very most out of life.

Louis de Louk writes about it in the simple little verse:

> A baby smiled in its mother's face;
>   The mother caught it, and gave it then
> To the baby's father—*serious case*—
>   Who carried it out to the other men;
> And every one of them went straight away
> Scattering sunshine through the day.

One day, as an experiment, and for the sheer adventure of it, I followed a smile all day long for the purpose of writing an article about it for a magazine. I saw a newsboy smile at a man to whom he sold a newspaper. I followed that man down the street, saw him infect ten people in one square, then saw him get on a bus and smile at the conductor. The conductor walked through his bus and infected everybody in the bus except one man—and he was blind. I followed that businessman into the office building where he worked and saw him spread that contagion of that smile to six people who were standing waiting for an elevator. I slipped into the elevator and saw him hand that smile on to the elevator girl who smiled back. Before we were up to the tenth floor he had infected ten more people. When he stepped into his office I saw him infect the receptionist at the information desk. I sat down for ten minutes and watched that girl spread the infection to ten people. The girl smiled at me after I had been sitting there and asked me what I wanted. I asked to see the man whom I had followed; I said it was about an important matter. It was to tell him what had happened that morning when he caught that smile from the newsboy, and we had a good laugh together over the adventure. The businessman suggested that I invite the newsboy for lunch as his guest if I had the time. I had and I did. He was a surprised boy when he got the invitation but he accepted. I told the story to five hundred men at a Rotary Club luncheon—and started the contagion of smiles on a wider round. Try it!

"IT IS THE WORLD'S SUN!"

IT happened that I had the inestimable privilege of spending a whole day as the guest of Dr. Sun Yat-sen, the founder of the Chinese Republic—he who overthrew the Manchus and brought about the new China; he who was China's first president; and he who is even now worshiped in every

Chinese home, schoolhouse, and university, as the "George Washington of China."

In a brief visit such as I had, with the consciousness that I was talking to one of the great immortals of this earth, and with the feeling that I would never have that privilege again, we covered a lot of territory, some of which I have written in magazine articles and books. However, there was one statement which Sun Yat made to me which has been for many years hidden away in my notebooks and only resurrected in recent weeks for this book.

As we sat having tea in his home in the French concession of Shanghai, where he was then in exile, he told me of one visit he made to the United States to raise money for the revolution. He was in Denver, Colorado, and, as he could not sleep, he got up just before dawn and was looking out of a window of the Brown Palace Hotel when suddenly the great, round golden sun bulged its way above the eastern horizon.

"An overwhelming sense of homesickness swept over me, for that sunrise reminded me of innumerable sunrises I had seen in my own China when I was in hiding in the mountains, and I cried out in my loneliness: 'That is China's sun!' "

Continuing, he said: "Then just as suddenly another overwhelming thought came to me: 'No, that is not China's sun! That is the world's sun.'

"It was like a religious conversion; like that experience which came to your Paul on the Road to Damascus. It struck me with a sudden vision that the sun belongs to the whole world. It was not only China's sun—it was even Japan's sun. It was Russia's; South America's; it was Europe's sun. It was Turkey's sun; it was the whole world's sun! I date my international thinking from that sunrise in the United States.

"I had, for so many years, been absolutely absorbed in

33

the problems of China, with the overthrow of the Manchus, with the birth of the Chinese Republic, with the raising of money to carry on the revolution, with imprisonment and threats to my life, that I had been thinking in terms of China and China alone, as if there were no other people in no other nation on the face of this earth than my China. Then suddenly that immortal morning, with that great round, golden sun breaking its way above the eastern horizon of your nation in that mountain region of Denver, Colorado, I suddenly realized that it was the world's sun and not exclusively China's sun. It was at that moment that my international thinking began, and from that moment my great resolve was to make my own nation great and strong so that China could help to bring about a feeling that the whole world was one."

Those are the notes that I have in my battered notebook from as far back as 1919, and, as I look them over, I have the feeling that Sun Yat-sen antedated Wendell Willkie in his "One World" idea by more than two decades, that the global idea was born that far back in the heart of this great Christian statesman Sun Yat-sen

❖❖❖

"NO, I WON'T! HERE I COME!"

A LOVELY young mother in Asheville, North Carolina, Mrs. Lee Tuttle, was sitting in her living room one morning when she heard a scream from her three-year-old daughter Dianne—a scream of fright, indignation, and anger. The mother jumped to her feet and tore to the back of the house from whence came that scream.

When she reached the back porch she saw a little drama of life. A rowdy of a boy had stolen Dianne's croquet mallet and was making off with it. Dianne was standing at the

34

edge of the alley at the back of the house yelling at the boy; "You bring my mallet back or I'll tell my mother!"

Then, as she saw her mother at the door, Dianne suddenly stopped in her tracks, put her hands defiantly on her hips in an attitude of belligerency, and seemed suddenly to change her mind. It seemed like a resolution to depend on herself rather than on her mother, and she yelled at the boy: "No, I won't! Here I come!"

And with that she doubled up her little fists, put her head down, like a goat, and made a run for the boy. She hit him in the stomach with both fists and head, knocked him flat on his back, grabbed her croquet mallet, and ran for home.

The afternoon of the day I heard that story I found myself saying over and over to myself: "No, I won't! Here I come! No, I won't! Here I come!" echoing that young valiant's sudden decision to look after herself and depend upon her own courage, prowess, and fists to retrieve her mallet. I have seldom heard a phrase that heartened me so much.

For that is exactly the spirit we need in American life at this particular juncture. American farmers, industrialists, laborers—anybody and everybody in this nation needs that spirit of Dianne, for we have come to depend too much upon subsidies, paternalism, and outside help to recover our lost toys, possessions, and rights.

We used to call the child who was always yelling to his parents for help a "sissy." We will have to watch carefully or we will get to be a "sissy" nation, for the tendency for many years has been for great groups in American life to depend upon helps and subsidies, far unlike the spirit of the pioneering ancestors who discovered and founded this nation.

But in any case, no matter whether you agree with me or

not as to the social or industrial application of Dianne's spirit, you will agree with me in its individual application. We know that it is wise to inculcate the spirit of Dianne into the hearts of our own children and our youth. They simply must learn to take care of themselves, to fight their own battles and make their own way without calling on their parents for help.

❖❖❖

AT HOME

ONCE I had dinner in the home of an admiral whom I have known for thirty years, and who had a heroic part in World War II. He was home on a leave, just as any ordinary gob would be. His son, a gob, was home at the same time.

During the dinner the son got to kidding his father, and finally the father, slightly irritated and no little discomfited by his son's repartee, suddenly turned on him, facetiously, and said with a smile: "Young man, you seem for the moment to have forgotten that I am your superior officer, considerably superior in fact."

The son's eyes twinkled and the rest of us waited expectantly for his repartee. This was his reply: "You may be an admiral in the Navy, but at home you are just my Pop."

We all had a good laugh and so did the admiral. But when I returned home I got into my letter files and unearthed a clipping that a soldier friend had sent me from London and which he thought I would like to keep. It seems that a London magazine had asked its subscribers for definitions of a home. They received over five thousand answers to that inquiry. Out of those, six were selected as the best and here they are:

Home—a world of strife shut out; a world of love shut in.

Home—a place where the small are great, and the great are small.

Home—the father's kingdom, the mother's world, and the child's paradise.

Home—the place where we grumble the most and are treated the best.

Home—the center of our affection, around which our heart's best wishes twine.

Home—the place where our stomachs get three square meals a day and our hearts a thousand.

HOW MANY INTERESTS HAVE YOU?

FOR several winter and summer seasons I had the privilege of being out on the same Chautauqua and lyceum circuit with Helen Keller. I came to know her well, and in spite of the fact that she was blind, deaf, and dumb, through her teacher Miss Sullivan she could answer questions and carry on an exciting open forum period. She had attained to a true philosophy of living which, curiously enough, fits into the needs of these times marvelously.

One day she was asked this question by a man in the audience: "How do you hope to approach old age?"

This is the answer that Helen Keller gave, as far as I can remember it from having put it down in my notes at the time:

You are the first person who has asked me point-blank how I intend to approach old age. Age seems to me only another physical handicap, and it excites no dread in me—I who have lived so long and so triumphantly with many limitations.

Once I had a dear friend of eighty who impressed upon me the fact that he enjoyed life more at eighty than he had at twenty. He used to say to me, "Never count how many years you have, but how many interests you have. Do not stale up your days by taking for granted the people around you, or the things which make up your environment, and you will ever abide in a realm of fadeless beauty and youth and life."

Then and there I resolved, vestal-like, to cherish an inextinguishable flame of youth. I have tried to avoid ruts—doing things just because my ancestors did them before me, leaning on the crutches of vicarious opinion, losing my childhood sense of wonderment. I am glad I still have a vivid sense of delight in new things and a vivid curiosity about the world I live in.

Age, I suppose, like blindness, is an individual experience. Everybody discovers its roseate mountain peaks, or its gloomy depths, according to his or her temperament. It is as natural for me, certainly, to believe that the richest harvest of happiness comes with old age, as that true sight and hearing are within, not without. Confidently I climb the broad stairway that love and faith have built to heights where I shall "attain to a boundless reach of sky."

Any person who comes to mid-life is constantly made aware of old age through the death of his friends and the great men and women of the earth whose passing is news to all humanity.

However, when all is said and done, if we have enough interests in life, as that wise woman Helen Keller says, we shall live a full, exciting and adventuring life up to the very end. That is the secret of growing old gracefully and happily. Browning was right when he said that immortal word:

> Grow old along with me!
> The best is yet to be,
> The last of life, for which the first was made.

How many interests have you, friend?

"WITHOUT MUCH LOVING CARE"

A FRIEND of mine sent me a poem which was written by a six-year-old girl in his Sunday school. The teacher of that class had wisely offered a prize for the best poem to be written, and this little girl handed in her poem. Here it is:

> Friendship is like a garden
> Of flowers rich and rare;
> It cannot reach perfection
> Without much loving care.

To me that poem is one of the most beautiful I have ever read, not only because of the unusual fact that a six-year-old child wrote it but also because of the eternal truth that is contained within its brief four lines. Within those lines lies the greatest truth on what to do with friendship, how to preserve it, how to make it rich and beautiful.

Now and then I see beautiful friendships broken for the simple reason that one party to that friendship does absolutely nothing to cultivate it. He simply accepts that friendship as if it, by divine right, belonged to him. He acts as if he had absolutely no responsibility in keeping that friendship watered, cultivated, and beautiful. I have seen hundreds of friendships wither and die for the simple lack of attention. I have seen many homes break up simply because one partner in that marriage did not take the trouble to try to keep it going, to speak a friendly, appreciative word which would be as water to a thirsty flower in that home. "The soul too must be fed and watered," I have heard some wise person say.

The wonder to me is that any friendship survives the neglect that many of us give to the garden of friendship and the flowers therein.

The little girl instinctively knew what she was writing

about. Friendship is a garden of flowers and it must be tended if it is to grow into beautiful blossoms. A flower will die if it does not get attention and any friendship will do the same thing.

I once wrote a book which I called *More Sermons in Stories.* I dedicated it to Clay Doss, who was then head of all sales for the Ford Motor Company, but who is now in the same capacity as vice-president of the Nash Company in charge of sales. Clay Doss has long been one of the dearest friends of my life. When I sent that book out into the world I wanted to tell him how much I valued his long time friendship so I dedicated the book to him in these four lines:

> And always when the old year ends
> I clasp my rosary of friends,
> And pause to breathe a grateful prayer
> For every bead of friendship there.

That was my simple, sincere way of watering the garden of friendship, hearkening to the admonition of that little six-year-old girl:

> Friendship is like a garden
> Of flowers rich and rare;
> It cannot reach perfection
> Without much loving care.

❖❖❖

"YOU GOT THERE!"

I WAS on a speaking trip of two weeks with the famous Dr. Frederick Norwood, who perhaps has had a more successful and spectacular preaching career than any minister in the English-speaking world.

He first became known and had a successful career for twenty-five years on the Australian continent. Then he went to City Temple in London and had an outstanding ministry in that great church and city during World War I. At that time he helped weld together England and Australia and interpreted each to the other. Now at seventy years of age, he is the pastor of a great church in Montreal, Canada, and doing splendidly. His career has covered three continents.

Perhaps this story which he told me on that trip will illustrate why he has been so uniformly successful.

It seems that when he was a young preacher in Sydney he was invited to preach in a small church about two hundred miles "up in the bush," as he discribed it to me.

He missed the only train in a week that would get him there, but nevertheless he started out to get there in time to preach as he had promised. The first eight miles he traveled on a bicycle. Then his bicycle broke down and he walked sixty miles. Then he met a traveler who was driving a wagon and went with him another hundred miles in a pouring rainstorm. The roads were so badly washed out that even the farmer could not go a mile farther, so this young preacher walked again for fifty miles, finally arriving on foot to keep his engagement.

Thirty years passed, and one day in London during World War I he met a group of Australian officers at a social event. When they heard his name one of them said: "Do you remember coming up into the bush to preach in a small country church in Australia a long time ago?"

"Yes, I remember it well for I had such a hard time to get there."

"Well, I was a small boy in that church and I shall never forget it, for we had looked forward for so long to your coming, and then you wired us that you had missed the train—but that you would still try to make it."

"Yes, I remember that, but I am surprised that you

remember it. Now let's see if you remember anything else about that trip. Do you remember, for instance, what I preached about that day?"

"No, I don't remember what you preached about nor your text nor anything else—but I do remember that you got there!"

Dr. Norwood tells me that three separate times in his life since that day he has run across people who remembered that preaching trip of over two hundred miles which he took up into the Australian bush. One day in Wimbledon he was attending the tennis matches and was particularly interested in a young Australian tennis star. After the game he asked to meet him. They got to talking, and when the boy heard Dr. Norwood's name, he said: "I shall never forget your name, for you were the young preacher who walked and bicycled and rode on a wagon two hundred miles to meet an engagement up in the bush."

Another time a couple came into his church in Montreal to be married. When they heard his name an old man in the party said: "I remember you well, for you were that young Australian minister who traveled two hundred miles by bicycle, horse, and shanks' mare to meet a speaking engagement in the bush."

"THANK YOU, GENTLEMEN!"

TWO women missionary friends of mine were traveling through bandit-infested sections of China. As their boat crept along the river toward Chentu, the captain became aware that they were being followed along the shore by bandits. The two missionary women became aware of the anxiety of the captain and asked what the trouble was.

"Bandits have been killing and robbing in this district. They know that you two women are on board and they

42

have been following us for hours along the shore. And we must tie up at the next pier."

As they made fast the boat to the pier they saw the bandits approaching stealthily, and the boatmen got out their long knives, prepared to fight for their lives.

Suddenly one of the missionary women cried out: "Captain! Put the gangplank down, I'm going ashore!"

The captain started to protest, but she jumped to the dock, and as the fierce-looking bandits approached she bowed low to the leader.

The leader, a great burly fellow looked puzzled, and then returned her bow.

"Thank you, gentlemen," the missionary said, smiling, "thank you for coming!"

The outlaws looked at her smiling face, bewildered and puzzled.

"We heard that there were bandits in this country," went on the missionary, "and we have been very much frightened. Now that you have come we know that we are safe, and we are grateful to you for coming to protect us."

The leader of the gang turned to his companions with a wide grin. They grinned in return and nodded, as the leader replied to the woman missionary: "We are gentlemen, as you have said. There is nothing to fear. We shall stand guard and you will be safe as long as we are caring for you!"

All night long that gang of bandits squatted with their guns across their knees beside the boat of the two women missionaries. And in the morning they went on their way, leaving them bowing and grinning on the pier.

This happens to be a true story of a universal psychology —that if you trust even the roughest persons, and assume that they are kindly and protective, there is a tendency for them to respond to that treatment and become what you

43

assume that they are. This is true of children, youth, and adults.

❖❖❖

THAT WAS A MOTHER'S WAY

ONE of my students who had come back from service in Europe as a chaplain once told me about a bombardment by the robot bombs on Liége, Belgium. The bombardment lasted all of one night, and in the morning hundreds of buildings were in ruins, with many people dead and dying under the heavy stones. Everybody in Liége worked frantically for many days to get the wounded and dead out of the cellars and streets where the huge stones had fallen on them. You could hear feeble cries for help for several days.

One day this young chaplain was working in a cellar on the main street where they could hear the feeble cries of a child begging for water. Over and over again that child cried out for water. He had been in the ruins four days and nights, in bitter cold weather, but when they finally got down to him they found him still alive and still crying for water. It seemed nothing short of a miracle that the child had survived that awful, crashing weight of stone, the bitter cold, and lack of food and water for four days and nights, but they found him still conscious, and with very few serious wounds.

While the chaplain was telling me the story he had a strange look in his eyes, almost a look of triumph when I asked him: "How in the world did that boy survive that crushing weight of stone and the four days and nights of terror? One would think that his body would have been crushed by the fallen stones of that old house."

"It was a miracle!" replied my student.

"What kind of a miracle?" I asked.

44

"A miracle of mother love, devotion, and sacrifice," he replied with tears in his frank and direct blue eyes.

"Yes—tell me about it."

"When we found that boy after digging for four days there he lay with his mother's own body curved over and above him like an arch, protecting him from the weight of the stones above him and keeping his body warm enough to survive all that time. If I ever saw a miracle of mother love that was it. She had deliberately curved her strong body over and above her child, taking the full brunt of the weight on her own body, and had died to save his life. I never saw anything as Christlike in my life. It was like that couplet you are always quoting to us from John Masefield:

> Oh, mother, when I think of thee,
> 'Tis but a step to Calvary."

"I guess you're right, son. Sacrifice is the usual spirit of motherhood."

✦✦✦

TURNING A MIRROR INTO A WINDOW

CHINA has an ancient parable that tells of a certain egotistical king who would dress up in his uniform, put on all his decorations, most of which were worthless, and strut up and down in front of a large mirror in his room to admire himself.

He was useless as a king, for he thought only of himself, his raiment, his power, and his own ego. He let his subjects starve to death, and the appalling neglect of his kingdom caused much misery. He might have been a good king if he had given less thought to himself and interested himself in his kingdom and the condition of his subjects.

One of his attendants, a wise old man who had been a member of the court for many years and an attendant of the king's father before him, realizing that the young king had possibilities if he would only think of something besides himself, came in the night and cut a window in the wall where the king's mirror stood, a window which would enable the king to look out into the street where his subjects passed by in their abject poverty.

When the self-centered monarch dressed up in his uniform and all the medals the next morning he walked to where the mirror had been, and saw, instead, his people passing in unending procession on the street. He saw a weary mother with her children dragging along in desperation and despair. He saw starving and slow-footed children, some reaching into garbage cans for crusts that might be there. He saw tired men, fathers of these children. He saw even a beautiful maiden of his own kingdom who caught his interest.

Suddenly he tore his medals from his breast, removed his ornate uniform, called for simple clothes, and hurried out into the street to mingle with his people. He discovered then their hunger, despair, and needs—even their blind affection for him. He even discovered for himself a beautiful wife.

The moment his mirror had been changed into a window he saw something besides his vain, self-worship, and he became a good king, a kindly person, a much-loved monarch, and he transformed his kingdom into a happy place to live. And I believe that if many of us changed our mirrors into windows we would be kinder, more lovable, and more loving and compassionate with our fellow men. We could look out and around us, rather than in; and we would think of others more than of ourselves.

❖❖❖

GALLANTRY IS NOT ALL DEAD

JOHNNY HUGHES, one of our American pilots, was shot down over Germany. He fought a good fight and had accounted for several German planes when his own ship, badly battered, was disabled. He was forced to bail out.

It was his first parachute jump in combat. In his highly nervous state he pulled the rip cord too soon and found himself floating in space, a perfect target for the circling German planes at ten thousand feet.

A fast German Messerschmitt circled closer and closer to him. Each circle of the plane brought the pilot nearer to Johnny for a good shot at him. Momentarily expecting to feel the ping of machine-gun bullets in his back, he gave himself up and offered final prayers for himself. He felt a twinge of self-pity, a deep throb of regret at having to give up his life. He thought of his mother, his sweetheart in Virginia, and steeled himself for the impact of bullets as he helplessly tossed in the wind, his parachute billowing in the blue sky above him, like a beautiful full-blooming flower in the wind against the blue heaven.

Resigning himself to the impact of bullets and death, his eyes, almost completely dazzled by the glaring sun, caught a gesture of chivalry as the German pilot's hand went stiffly to his cap in salute to a valiant foe and the German plane zoomed off toward the Rhineland.

Johnny hopes that he may meet the German pilot some day to express his thanks for sparing his life, and for his gallantry. Johnny Hughes has never forgotten the smile and gallant salute! He can never believe that all Germans are cruel.

It is Johnny's idea, in which I share, that whenever we hear a story of that type we should pass it on, for it is not unreasonable to hope that there are many good and gallant men in Germany as well as in our own nation. They are not all supermen and they are not all monsters. In fact, Ted Malone, one of my favorite radio broadcasters from the war zone, came up with a story of a visit he had made to two German prison camps, one for women and one for men, and he said: "I must be fair enough to report that the inmates of those two camps had been treated fairly and fed well, and had few real complaints to make against the Germans, all things taken into consideration."

In all fairness I would like to relate a statement made by a returned missionary to China told me in Boston. She said that one evening in occupied China there was a knock at their missionary compound door and there stood a Japanese major. He bowed politely and said: "I understand that you are having a prayer meeting here tonight. I am also a Christian and I would like to kneel with you and have a part in your prayer meeting. I would be killed if it were discovered that I am here but I am hungry for fellowship with Christians. I hate this war and shall protect you Christians to the best of my ability."

This actually happened, and is in no way a story for propaganda. My friend was the woman to whom it happened and it cannot be gainsaid. I tell it because we hear much of cruelty on the part of the Japanese. Now and then we hear a story like that from authentic sources, and it is our duty to tell it. The only hope we have is the hope that there are enough people like these left in Germany and Japan to work with for the future peace of the world.

"WITH LIGHTNING-LIKE SPEED"

H. G. WELLS was truly a great writer. All his life he not only interpreted the contemporary scenes of life in such

48

books as *Mr. Britling Sees It Through,* a story of World War I, but was also a prophet in his books, giving us pictures of the world to come. However, he was best known for his colossal *Outline of History.*

One day a critic asked him if he looked upon himself as a prophet, to which he replied with typically Wellsian compactness: "No, I'm not a prophet. I simply run as fast as I can beside the marching procession of life, pointing to it as it moves with lightning-like speed into the future."

What a true picture of our rapidly moving life that is. When we think of what has happened in one generation—airplanes that swoop from city to city, and nation to nation in a few hours. Once I flew from Washington, D. C., to Miami, Florida, and made it in four hours, with a tail wind. The next week I took a train on the same route, and it took me more than twenty-four hours to make the trip back from Miami to Washington. My lyceum bureau scheduled me to go by bus and train on my next lecture trip from Rochester, New York, to Corning, New York. I hopped on a plane and flew over in forty minutes.

Radio, airplanes, insulin, penicillin, the sulfa drugs. The world is changing overnight. A man eats breakfast in London, has dinner in New York, talks with Generalissimo Chiang Kai-shek on Monday and with President Truman on Wednesday. It's a bewildering, swift-moving, appalling procession that we are in. We have little time to prophesy. We have time only to point to the swiftly moving procession of life.

As each year passes into history and we face a new year, we wonder if the new year will hold such miracles as the passing year brought forth, and the answer is that it will.

John Crummey, president of Food Machinery Company, visited me at my home. He was negotiating the purchase of a potato-peeling machine which takes off the skin as thin as tissue paper, digs out the eyes, and paints the peeled potatoes with a thin edible white coating. He told me that within a few years all potatoes will be marketed prepeeled and coated and packed in bags. Yes, we are moving fast— and this year will be no exception, friends!

❖❖❖

"ONLY THAT DAY DAWNS TO WHICH WE ARE AWAKE"

AMONG countless wise sayings of Henry Thoreau is the utterance he once made: "Only that day dawns to which we are awake."

How true that is of even the physical dawns. One of the great tragedies of human life is the innumerable sunrises that the city dweller, and even the country dweller, never sees because he is still sleeping soundly and misses them. The birds are wiser than we; they greet the dawns with a song and then go back to bed again, but they are always up to see the splendor of each dawn and they welcome it with a chorus of song. The story of Rostand's *Chantecler* set this into immortal and unforgettable drama. Most of us miss the dawns because we are sound asleep, and as a result those days did not dawn for us. We missed them.

In larger matters—spiritual matters—this is especially true. Today a new world is dawning—a global world, an international family. But to him who is not awake to this great and splendid movement of human thinking it is as though it were not. "Only that day dawns to which we are awake."

From an author, whose name I do not know, I quote two of my favorite lines: "He looked importantly about him while all the world went on without him." That is another way of saying the simpler statement of Thoreau: "Only that day dawns to which we are awake."

50

I talked with a boy who had just come back from Iran. He was trying to tell a group about the importance of knowing, liking, and co-operating with Russia. The listeners were resisting his arguments, indifferent to them, or just much uninformed about Russia. Living and working with the Russians for two years, the lad had learned not only to respect them but to love them. He claimed that they are closer to us in spirit than anybody on this earth. His statements of his experiences were made in absolute faith in the Russian people. You see, he had been in Russia and had lived with the Russians. The group seemed worse than indifferent; they were belligerent and totally unacquainted with the Russian people. They had never bothered to read about Russia, with whom we will have to learn to live to keep the peace of the world. They refused to listen with open minds, were unimpressed; and I was struck with the boy's utter helplessness when he turned to me and said (because I had shown a desire to learn more about Russia) : "These guys just won't be informed. They don't want to know!" This battle-scarred boy was trying to tell me in his own boyish way: "Only that day dawns to which we are awake." I believe he was right.

A whole new world is awakening. There is a new era of missionary work dawning; there is a whole new global world dawning, but only that day dawns to which we are awake, and the nation, the people, the church, which does not even know that such a new day is dawning—that nation, that people, that church, will be left in the backwash of history.

❖❖❖

"TO HELP HIM PLOUGH A PERFECT LINE"

BROWSING through John Masefield's *The Everlasting Mercy* I caught a few lines that thrilled me. It was the word picture of Saul Kane, the converted prize fighter who had gone to the country to escape his old, hampering environment, and to live a clean, Christian life. He was put to work ploughing a field and these two lines were descriptive of his ploughing:

> His eyes forever on some sign
> To help him plough a perfect line.

What a picture that is to some of us who, as boys, had to plough a perfect line and whose fathers taught us to keep an eye on a tree, a fence post, or a rock at the end of our furrow to help us plough a perfect line.

I want to add to that couplet a legend I recently found, a story of a man who had allowed himself to become stooped before his time. He decided to have a friend who was a sculptor make a statue of himself which was to be perfectly straight, with the shoulders as stiff as a ramrod, and body unbent. The sculptor completed the statue and then the stooped man hid it away in his garden in an inaccessible spot, and every day he would visit the spot and stand for a few minutes looking at it. Unconsciously he would straighten up during those minutes that he contemplated himself as straight and tall and true physically.

After a few months his friends noticed that he even walked more erect and the old stoop of the shoulders seemed to have at least partially disappeared.

One day his little granddaughter saw her "Da," as she called him, going off in the woods, and curious as to what his errand might be, she followed him down the path to his secret place. She saw her grandfather gazing at what seemed to be another "Da" made of bronze and could not comprehend the meaning of it. She was awed and more than a little frightened as she saw her grandfather looking at himself, as it seemed to her. Holding her breath she stood as though rooted to the spot, watching the mysterious scene.

Then she noticed something which suddenly took her child-mind off the first wonder—and that was that her grandfather, who was usually bent, stood up straight and tall and firm. Then it was that her childish control left her and she cried out with a great wonder in her heart and a ring of delight on her lips! "Da, Da! Why you're standing as straight as a tree! You're straight, Da!"

And he was! He had been so tremendously influenced by the statue of himself made by his sculptor friend that he had become an erect likeness of the statue through his admiration of the posture and constantly gazing at it.

In everyday life we contemplate, ponder, and admire, unaware that our mental functions are shaping our lives and our bodies. "As he thinketh in his heart, so is he" is an ancient, pithy saying of that experience.

"BUT THE ROADS ENDURE"

I HAVE always been interested in streets and roads. There are several immortal streets in great cities the world over. In Tokyo I have often strolled down the Ginza which has a personality all its own. In Berlin, Unter den Linden is the famous street, although the lindens have been uprooted and most of the buildings destroyed in World War II.

In Paris there is the Champs Elysées; in Shanghai, Bubbling Well Road; in San Francisco, Market Street; in Detroit, Woodward Avenue; and in Boston, Commonwealth Avenue. These streets are known in literature around the world.

In Samao there is the Road of the Loving Heart, which was built by native chiefs as a memorial to Robert Louis

Stevenson, who is buried on the island. The Romans were great road builders and left their mark all over Europe.

Road building has been a great art in war, and the ability of our Army to take bulldozers into a coral island and build perfect roads in a few days has been one of the principal reasons why we were able to win the Pacific war. We Americans are great road builders. Our continent is crossed and crisscrossed by the finest highway systems in the world, a road building ability which makes even Hitler's famous *Autobahn* look like the play road of a small boy working in sand on a summer beach.

Many of us who have had as a hobby transcontinental driving have come to know the famous American highways such as the Lincoln Highway, Nos. 22, 6, 91, and 10. They are like our own local highways. The Pennsylvania Turnpike, the Worcester Turnpike, the Pulaski Highway have become household words to travelers.

Now we hear tall talk of an Alaskan Highway which will give us all access to the wonders of that pioneer land, and of a highway to Mexico City, and of the South American Highway over which, in due time, we shall be able to travel the entire length of the South American continent.

All of which reminds me of Ethelyn Miller Hartwich's verse which has romance, history, and eternal truth in it, such truths as brings memories of biblical highways like the road to Damascus, the Emmaus highway, the Jericho road, and many others:

> Great roads the Romans built that men might meet,
> And walls to keep strong men apart, secure.
> Now centuries are gone, and in defeat
> The walls are fallen, but the roads endure.

❖❖❖

"SOMETHING WHICH WILL BRIGHTEN
ALL ETERNITY"

I REMEMBER hearing a bright young attorney in our town, Mr. Charles Carrigan, speak at an Elks memorial service. I was a high-school boy at the time, and the motto of the Elks organization impressed me: "The faults of our brothers we write upon the sands, their virtues upon the tablets of love and memory."

All through life I have carried that phrase in my memory to brighten and lighten my life, and I have quoted it ten thousand times, including this time. Forty years after I first heard it I had the pleasure of quoting it at a Rotary meeting in my home town, with Charlie Carrigan present, and told that assembled group that I had got it from him and that I had carried it around the earth in my public ministrations. He was naturally pleased and so was I.

I had filed away in my memory something that I added in my talk. The immortal Daniel Webster once said, when he was talking in a certain trial in New England:

If we work upon marble, it will perish. If we work upon brass, time will efface it. If we rear temples, they will crumble into dust. But if we work upon immortal souls, if we imbue them with principles, with the just fear of God and love of their fellowmen, we engrave on those tablets something which will brighten all eternity.

"Something which will brighten all eternity" is what another great orator was saying when he gave to people this high and holy thought: "A single great sentence may often outlive a marble temple."

And if you do not believe that statement is true, just dip into the Greek, Roman, and German poets and seers. Their immortal sayings still live while their temples and towers, minarets and domes have crumbled to dust and are forgotten. And that also is true of the Jews who gave us the Old Testament.

The only things which will live forever and brighten all eternity are those things which are engraved or written on the hearts of humanity, particularly upon the tablets of little children; they who have handed down the Mother Goose rhymes for centuries to adults.

❖❖❖

TALKERS AND FLIERS

BILL STOUT, the great aviation engineer of this generation, told me a story about Orville Wright, one of the famous Wright brothers, which is worth passing on for its humor, if not for its philosophy.

Orville Wright, in his early days, was once told by a well-wisher that he was too modest: "You don't assert yourself enough. You will have to learn to promote yourself, and, if not yourself, your ideas. You should have a press agent."

"Well," said Wright, after several moments of reflection, "the best talker and the worst flier among the birds is the parrot."

"All of which," added Bill Stout, "was very modest, very dignified, and very untrue; for if a man has a great idea that will benefit humanity, he has a right, even an obligation in some way to get that idea developed, manufactured, produced, and known. This is a day of promotion. Many a great idea has been laid on the shelf because its inventor had no way of getting it before the public. In spite of Orville Wright's clever story, promotion, publicity, and production are all vital to an inventor, an engineer, and a creator."

Bill Stout is right. We would likely have never had the jet propulsion airplane, the atomic bomb, the quick development of radar, the miracle drug penicillin, and the sulfa drugs if it had not been for the publicity and promotion which was brought to them. All of these modern creations might have lain dormant for fifty or one hundred years if it had not been for the impetus that came from war and a strong world-wide publicity which created an atmosphere in which scientists could work.

I have always said that the man who hands on to us a great poem, who quotes it, is as important in the chain of service as the man who wrote that poem. So it is with the man who calls our attention to a great motion picture, a great drama, a great book. Otherwise we might never see, hear, or read the picture, book, or poem. Therefore he who promotes is as important a factor in the chain of service as he who creates.

The newspaper editor, the preacher, the friend, the promotor, has his vital and important place in life. Advertising is as important as creating and writing and inventing in the modern scheme of living. The United States has gone to bat on this end of life and has done it well. And why not? Anything worth writing, inventing, or creating, is worth telling about, producing, and promoting.

Orville Wright may hold to his modesty, but there must be someone along the line who talks as well as flies, and this nation has produced a lot of people with talent in that realm. It is well for all of us that we have produced them. Nobody who is a good advertiser, promotor, and seller need be apologetic to an American who has been brought up in our day and in our ways.

❖❖❖

ALWAYS ABLE TO SEE THE STARS

IN one of A. J. Cronin's books the young hero has just arrived at a Scotch home to visit his sweetheart. The girl keeps him waiting, as is the way of all sweethearts, while she is polishing her fingernails, rouging her cheeks, and putting on lipstick, making herself perfectly presentable in order to make the best impression possible when she comes downstairs.

During the time she was doing her final chore of "homework" the mother had to entertain the boy downstairs, and in order to make conversation the mother said to the boy: "How is the weather outside?"

The young man replied: "It's a bit misty but you can still see the stars."

"Robert, *you* will always be able to see the stars!" she replied.

That dialogue reminds me of something that Santayana, the great Harvard philosopher, said to the American soldiers who took over the city of Rome in World War II. When they entered Rome they found Santayana in a monastary, peaceful, secure, and satisfied. He seemed perfectly poised and undisturbed by the turmoil, and disturbance of the war. He was evidently untouched with its privations, bombings, and dangers. One of the American soldiers asked him how it was that he could keep right on working at a book while the whole city was under bombardment, and turbulence reigned in everybody else's heart. This is what Santayana replied:

"The dismay that has fallen on so many minds has not touched me because I live in the Eternal."

Which was exactly the spirit of Lincoln in the Civil War when Edwin Stanton asked him practically the same question, and Lincoln replied: "A man doesn't worry much when he feels that he is only a pipe for omnipotence to sound through."

❖❖❖

"THE MIND OF AN ANGEL, AND THE SOUL OF A SEER"

I HAVE written at other times of the great man to whom the title of this story was applied, and I have written about him because I once spent an hour with him in the General Electric laboratories in Schenectady, New York. Most of my readers know who he is but they do not know out of what a terrible environment and with what terrific physical handicaps he battled all of his eventful days.

In 1865 a crippled, misshapen child was born in Breslau, Germany. His father and grandfather had a serious spinal trouble and that affliction had been passed on to this child. One tragedy after another befell the poor German lad. When he was only a year old his mother died. When he reached childhood it became certain that his awful deformity could never be corrected. Down to the end of his days he would be a physical weakling, deprived of normal contacts, play, and friendships. He would always be hideously ugly and repulsive to people who did not know his great heart and mind.

In addition to that, he knew that he would never be free from a constant pain in every movement of his body. That was not all. After the boy had made his way through college and university, in spite of his terrible physical handicap, and was just about to receive his coveted degree, the German authorities became suspicious of what they called his radical tendencies. So he had to leave Germany and become an exile from his home. He did this as secretly as he could, going first to Switzerland, the historic haven of all refugees from Germany.

In 1889 the young cripple, friendless, distrusted, and desperately poor, reached New York, traveling to the land of hope in steerage on an immigrant liner which took more than a month to make the voyage which airplanes now make in less than a day. Hundreds of those poor immigrants, sturdier far than this boy, died on that terrible voyage. It was his hope, his faith, his courage, and his mind that kept this crippled boy alive to reach the "Melting Pot of the World," this land of hope.

At long last the gates of this new world swung open to him; the Statue of Liberty arose on the port bow of this immigrant ship and big tears rolled down his swarthy cheeks unheeded. That boy was Charles Steinmetz, and he made himself, in the years that followed, one of the world's leaders in electrical engineering. People called him "a hunchback who played with thunder and lightning."

When he died in 1923 scientists from the whole world vied to do him honor. He had made a greater contribution to electrical engineering than any other human being, a contribution that a thousand times has helped us to wage and win the world wars which were started by the very German spirit that drove him from that land in the first place. So he has had his revenge, if there was ever any revenge in his gentle, tender, universal heart, which those of us who knew him doubt.

Indeed one editorial in the New York Times said of him at his death: "This deformed hunchback had the body of a cripple, the mind of an angel, and the soul of a seer."

Thousands of men returned from World War II crippled and deformed. They too will have to face the handicaps that this hunchback faced; only most of them will face lesser evils than he faced. What an inspiration that little hunchback will be to the deformed, legless, eyeless men who have returned from the war to make their way in a new world as he did.

❖❖❖

"WHAT ABOUT MARY?"

I ONCE read a story about a truly great person which stirred me deeply.

A certain group of young people were talking about the great personalities of this day and age.

One adult said: "Well, there's President Roosevelt, Prime Minister Churchill, Marshal Stalin, Chiang Kai-shek, General Eisenhower, and General MacArthur."

"And Mary!" one little boy interjected.

"Mary? Who is Mary?" the elder asked, a little peeved by the interruption of the small boy.

"Oh, you know—Mary—Mary?"

And then the interesting game which was being played by one adult and several children as to who were the truly great of the earth turned into a query as to who this "Mary" was.

It turned out that Mary was a beautiful, simple, humble, red-haired girl, who was a cashier at a certain restaurant. Her smile was young every morning and was still going well at night. If a man was cross, grouchy, peevish when he came in, Mary's smile warmed his heart, and before he left that restaurant he was happy and smiling. All you had to do was just to look at Mary's smile and you were transformed, no matter how low you felt when you entered the restaurant.

Nobody could go into that restaurant, even in the saddest, bluest, rainiest day and not be transformed by Mary's pleasant ways, words, and smiles. She loved everyone and they all loved Mary. She was like a spring morning, like sunshine breaking through a dark cloud, like a song, a hymn, a child's laughter.

When you entered that restaurant filled with the cares of earth, with a loneliness on you because your boy was in France, or your husband was in the South Seas, or your

61

father was in the Philippines, and Mary smiled at you, you wanted to sing "O what a beautiful morning, O what a beautiful day—Everything's going my way." That was what Mary did to, and for, you.

Even little children loved to go into that restaurant with their parents because Mary always made a fuss over them, saw that they got an extra cake, and that they got, what is even more important, a little attention. It made them feel grown up. That's Mary's way and it had been as far back as anybody could remember, and yet through all the years Mary seemed to keep perpetually young because of what was happening inside her soul.

So in that little group where the game was being played of selecting the names of the most important people in contemporary life, and several had espoused Mary's cause by telling some of the kindly things she had done for them, suddenly Mary's little advocate spoke up with a note of authority: "Well, what about Mary? Is she important or isn't she important?"

The adult who was directing this game replied: "Well, let me begin all over again, Bobby, and name the great of the earth. There's Roosevelt, Churchill, Stalin, Chiang Kaishek, Marshall, Eisenhower, McArthur—"

"Is Roosevelt more important than Mary?" Bobby insisted.

❖❖❖

"I ALWAYS DO HANG OUT A FINE WASHING"

A GREAT English minister used to tell a good story which illustrates the way all of us should be doing whatever humble chore come to us.

On Monday morning Dr. F. B. Meyer, who told me the story, was taking his usual Monday morning walk to get the cobwebs out of his brain and the weariness out of his soul. In his walk he passed by the humble cottage of an old parishioner. She was hanging her Monday morning wash on the line. The clothes looked white and well washed and Dr. Meyer, more in fun than anything else, said to her: "You certainly hang out a fine wash, Mrs. Jones!"

She replied with the pride of fine workmanship in her voice: "I always do hang out as fine a looking wash as anybody on this street, if I do say it that shouldn't."

That's the spirit, friends. The old English mother accepted the humble task assigned by fate and took it seriously. She was not concerned with affairs of state, war strategy, big business, or important affairs, but what she had to do she did well, taking a pride in her chore. That is the spirit, not only in personal life and living, but it is the way to get the most out of life always.

❖❖❖

"AND I AM READY TO DEPART"

FOR many years Edwin Markham, the great American poet, and I used to talk for long hours together about his favorite this and that. I was in the process of writing his biography and it was my duty to discover his favorite hymn, poetry, food, and what have you. So from time to time I would ask him pointed questions.

One morning, standing on the rim of the Grand Canyon, I asked him how it impressed him and he said: "It makes me think of my favorite quotation."

"What is your favorite quotation, Mr. Markham?" I asked him.

He replied:

> That's the wise thrush; he sings each song twice over,
> Lest you should think he never could recapture
> The first fine careless rapture!

"Who wrote it?" I asked.

"Browning," was his reply.

That brought us to the subject of poetry and then he told me what his favorite quatrain was. I had forgotten it for years until recently, when I read Maugham's novel *The Razor's Edge* and found Mr. Markham's favorite quatrain quoted by a character in that book. The quatrain was written by Walter Savage Landor and reads:

> I strove with none, for none was worth my strife;
>> Nature I loved; and next to Nature, Art.
> I warm'd both hands against the fire of life;
>> It sinks, and I am ready to depart.

Since reading that quatrain in *The Razor's Edge* I have carried out a lifelong intention and memorized it. I have never memorized a quotation which I use more than that one. Mr. Markham called it the greatest quatrain in the English language and my guess is that the good gray poet was right. It has more in its compact four lines than any poem I know. It helps me to get more out of life by saying it over to myself. It is particularly enriching for those of us who have come to the mid-years of life.

❖❖❖

"BECAUSE IT IS THERE!"

JUST before Rear Admiral Richard E. Byrd sailed on his last trip of exploration to the Antarctic I interviewed him at his home on Brimmer Street in Boston, and one of the questions I asked him was: "Just why are you making this perilous trip, Admiral Byrd?"

His reply is one of the immortal answers to such foolish questions. This is what he replied:

"I can answer your question in the same way that such a question was answered by one of the Englishmen who climbed Mount Everest, to their death, as it turned out. When he was asked by a curious reporter why he was climbing Mount Everest he replied: 'Because it is there!' I think that is as good an answer as I can make to your question. I am going to the Antarctic because it is there, because it challenges me, because it is still unknown, unexplored, and unconquered. Such a spot is always a challenge to an explorer. There are so few places left on this earth that are unexplored that we explorers are running out of adventure. If we don't take every opportunity we will be among the unemployed. I am going just because it is there!"

I put that answer from this great explorer down in my notes because I have the feeling that it is about as fine an answer as I have ever heard to such a question.

We Americans have done the impossible in creating, building, and flying airplanes. We have done it because the need was there to make faster, heavier, and safer planes. Jet propulsion has been a challenge to our designers for half a century. It was there to be explored and exploited and we have done it. The need was there and the possibility was there. That was sufficient challenge to us.

The white crest of untrod Mount Everest was there a perpetual challenge to the spirit of man and he accepted it. The unconquered air spaces of the universe were there as a perpetual challenge to the spirit of man and he accepted that challenge and the miracles have come to pass.

Certain universal diseases are there: cancer, infantile paralysis, tuberculosis, the venereal diseases, and they have been a perpetual challenge to the spirit of man. He is meeting that challenge and discovering, inventing, creating, developing, and manufacturing the sulpha drugs, penicillin, and hormones—all of them miracles of the medical profession and the laboratories.

The very fact that some disease is there seems to be an insidious enemy of mankind is enough to challenge him to conquer that enemy. That is all that mankind needs: the fact that the disease is there.

"Thou hast made him a little lower than the angels" seems to have been aptly said of humankind. "Man—stands he not at the center of immensities, at the conflux of two externities?" is also a wise word said by Thomas Carlyle. He is made just a little lower than the angels and he stands at the center of immensities and those immensities challenge the godlike spirit with which he is endowed. Therefore there is nothing too large for him, no danger too great to baffle his spirit. He is unconquerable; he is unflinching.

"HOW TO BE HAPPY WITHOUT HATE"

"I HAVE a lot of men with whom I am friends because we hate the same people." So said a friend who has a facetious mood now and then.

Fortunately I happen to know that the man who made that remark doesn't hate anybody, and I am glad to add that statement to the opening paragraph of this little piece. No man or woman can be entirely happy who hates anybody in any place at any time. Hate drives out happiness. It is the expulsive power of an old disaster. Only those who have driven hate out of their souls with love are entirely happy in this life.

When I was a boy, living in West Virginia, my father often said to me: "Never say anything about a man if you cannot say something good. Never think a mean thing about a man if you can possibly think a good thing about him."

I usually try to live up to the precepts of my wise father, but now and then I have my moments of weakness, and in those moments I always lay up for myself hours, days, and even weeks—often months—of unhappiness and misery. I am naturally not a hater. No human being is. That is contemporaneously illustrated by the way our American soldiers get along with our erstwhile enemies, the Japanese and Germans, even to marrying them. Within two months of the American occupation of Germany more than five hundred applications for marriages between American boys and German girls had been turned in. Even within two weeks after the capitulation of Japan our American boys were handing out chewing gum and candy to Japanese children, giving blood to Tojo, the Japanese prime minister who planned the Pearl Harbor attack, and had won the hearts of even adults in that faraway land. No, we Americans are never natural haters.

We find it easier to be happy without hating anybody on earth, we Americans, and that is the hope of the world.

When I was a student I had the exciting adventure of meeting Henry van Dyke, the famous poet from Princeton University. Later we had the pleasure of hearing his lecture in our town on the camp grounds. As a reporter for the *Moundsville Echo* I took it all down in shorthand, and later I memorized it. I shall never forget it. This is what Mr. van Dyke said about hate: "There are two good rules which ought to be written on every heart: Never believe anything bad about anybody unless you positively know it is true; never tell even that unless you feel that it is absolutely necessary and that God is listening while you tell it."

I was much impressed with this statement by Mr. van Dyke. I went home and told my father that I believed he was just as smart as Mr. van Dyke. He smiled.

"HOW CAN A MAN GIVE A BRAVE BLOW?"

A HUSBAND, even as you and I have so often done, was trying to hang a picture on the wall of the living room for his wife. Although he was standing on a chair he could not quite reach the desired spot.

His wife, who was directing the operation, placed a wiggly stool on top of the chair for additional height, from which her wobbly husband could work. Stepping on the stool and balancing himself precariously, the husband gave the nail a few timid, cautious, almost gentle taps with the hammer.

"Why don't you give a brave blow or two and settle it?" asked his wife petulantly.

"How can a man give a brave blow," replied the husband, "when he is standing on a foundation like this?"

That husband spoke wiser than he knew. The first essential for giving a brave blow is a solid foundation on which to stand in this life. It is true in personal life. The man who has a solid reputation, an unimpeachable character in any community, is the man who can draw back and take a hefty swing at anything he chooses to hit. But the man who does not stand on such a solid basis has to hit cautiously. The politician running for office who has a good reputation and nothing to hide is the man who can step out into public life unafraid, and strike a blow for justice and righteousness.

That is why, when a party caucus is selecting a man to run for office, it always looks into his past to see if there are hidden scandals or bad spots, for those smart politicians know that when a man runs for public office his entire past is likely to be aired to the public. They know also that if his past is not clean and immaculate, he will not strike any free, full blows for good, for his standing will be too vulnerable.

During the last year of World War II there was a good

deal of impatience on the part of the American public following the spectacular sweep of General Patton's army across France. The American public wondered why he didn't go right on across the Rhine in the same stride and with the same speed. However, General Eisenhower was too smart for that. Patton's lines of communications had been extended too far, his army was tired, his supplies limited. He stopped, reformed his army, waited for his supplies to catch up with him in sufficient quantities, and, when he had laid himself a solid enough foundation, he began giving the Germans some good solid, brave blows. If he had not waited until he was standing on a good solid foundation, he might have been driven back.

So is it in life. They are wise people who get a solid foundation to stand on first of all—the foundation of a good education, of preparation for life, of character, and integrity. Then and then only can anybody strike a brave blow and be sure that he himself will not tumble from his perch.

❖❖❖

CHICKENS COMING HOME TO ROOST

ONCE I entertained a handsome, six-foot-three young ensign at lunch in Boston. His ship was in for repairs at the Charleston Navy Yard. I noticed that all the girls in the restaurant kept shy eyes on him as we walked in and as we ate, and I didn't blame them, for he looked as if he had just stepped out of Hollywood—wholesome, virile, and handsome.

He was a Middle Western Methodist preacher's son, and the first thing he said to me as we sat down was: "My father said that if I didn't phone Bill Stidger in Boston I needn't come back to Nebraska again."

"So your father bulldozed you into coming to see me?"

"Yes, Doctor, but there was another reason of my very own why I wanted to see you."

"And what was that, son?"

"When I was four years old you came to lecture for my dad in Nebraska, and the first thing you did when you stepped into the house was to reach into your pocket and give me a package of Life Savers, and I have never forgotten you or that act of generosity. Every time I see a white life saver on my destroyer I smile and think of you."

I had forgotten that particular package, for I have been handing them out to children for a quarter of a century; and look upon myself as one of the chief markets of this delicious type of candy. I buy them by the box for the purpose of handing them out to children. I learned that fine art from Dr. Dillon Bronson, who all during his ministry used to carry in his pockets deflated rubber toy balloons and give them to the children. Once in San Jose, California, when he was filling my pulpit during World War I, he gave my daughter Betty a red balloon, as he did hundreds of the children in my church. When I came back to my pulpit I didn't hear much about his preaching, although he was a good preacher, but I did hear a lot about his giving away balloons to the children.

That inspired me to start my Life Savers crusade to win the hearts of children, and I have been at it ever since. And at long last I heard this young ensign tell me that he remembers me for that one act when he was a lad of four years. Thus some of my chickens of service have come home to roost, and my heart has been warmed and little songs are singing in my soul. I got a kick out of that.

❖❖❖

EARS TUNED TO THE CRY OF DISTRESS

BISHOP FRANCIS J. McCONNELL once told me a story of one of his vivid experiences on Cape Cod when he was a student preacher. He was walking one stormy night with an old sea captain along the shore. The captain was a patrol for the life guards, and he loved it. It was a wild, noisy, tempestuous night and each had to yell above the noise of the elements in order to be heard.

Suddenly the captain halted dead still in his tracks, cupped his hand to his ear, and said: "I hear a cry of distress out in the surf. Somebody is in trouble."

Bishop McConnell hadn't heard any cry of distress, but that old man's ears were tuned to a cry of distress and he had heard it. He reported it immediately to the life guards and, sure enough, they went out and rescued two fishermen who were clinging to an upturned boat.

I then told the good and great bishop a story to match his—for a fair exchange is no robbery.

A little child had been sick for several nights and her mother had tended her each night. But this one particularly hot summer night she had retired early for a much-needed rest. The windows being open, the clang and bang of two streetcar lines caused a terrible din but she slept on undisturbed. A fire engine swept by with its siren blowing full blast but her deep slumber was undisturbed. Boys, playing baseball in a next door lot, yelled and shouted, but she slept on, unconscious of what was happening around her. The telephone rang three times before the father answered it. He had been absorved in the radio baseball news. When it proved to be a wrong number call he let out a yell of indignation—then remembered his sleeping wife, tiptoed into her room, and smiled to himself when he saw that his roar had not disturbed her sleep, nor had the ringing phone. She was oblivious to all the noise.

He had hardly sat down again when the baby's voice in the back bedroom cried out feebly: "Mother! I want my mother!" In a flash that soundly sleeping mother was up, out of the room, and at her baby's side. She was not disturbed by the streetcars, fire engines, yelling boys, or ringing phone, but her ear was tuned to the cry of distress from her sick baby.

So the ears of the nation are tuned to the cry of distress from the hungry world, and we are answering that cry. We may have many faults as a nation, but our national ears have always been tuned to the world's cry of distress.

❖❖❖

A BOY AND AND HIS MARBLES

DR. HAROLD RUOPP, who is pastor of a large Chicago church, went to visit in Stoneham, Massachusetts, where he had formerly preached. While there he called on a friend of his, a paralytic, who ran a small hole-in-the-wall candy shop for children. The man kept candy, chewing gum, toys, marbles, and other small things that might interest the "small fry" of the town.

On the day that Dr. Ruopp visited his old friend a small boy about six years of age came into the shop and asked if there were any marbles. The owner pointed to a large jar full of brightly colored marbles on the counter.

"How much?" asked the small boy.

"Ten cents a dozen," responded the kindly storekeeper.

The boy stood in the middle of the small shop scratching his head. It was an apparent struggle between spending his ten cents for marbles or candy, which is always a small boy's problem.

"What's the matter, sonny, haven't you ten cents?" asked the gentle owner, who always understood the ways of small boys.

"Yes, sir," replied the boy, "but that's all I do have, sir!"

Dr. Ruopp, seeing the struggle which was going on, said: "Son, it just happens that I have a special marble fund, and here is a dime from the fund. You can have it and buy the marbles you want and still have a dime for candy." The boy hesitated, scratched his tousled head in bewildered astonishment, then took the proffered dime, walked over to the marble jar, a beautiful light shining in his eyes, and got his dozen marbles.

He thanked Dr. Ruopp, stood shyly for a moment, and then bolted for the door. As he went out he exclaimed, as with unbelieving heart, his astonishment, his gratitude and his joy: "Gee whiz!"

The two adults in the store laughed aloud over the delight of this investment of money in a small boy. They had hardly finished talking about it before their small friend returned, leading another boy by the hand. They were running.

"He's found a pal and is bringing him in to get another handout from an easy mark!" said the storekeeper with the usual adult cynicism.

"I guess that's it, and I don't blame him," said Dr. Ruopp.

They were both mistaken, for what actually happened was even more comforting and heartwarming than the first kindly deed. The boys stopped at the door and shyly peeked in, and the boy who had received the bounty of marbles said to his friend, pointing at Dr. Ruopp with boyish awe in his voice, almost like the Amen of a prayer: "That's him!" And off they ran as fast as their chubby little legs could carry them.

The denouement of this story is that Dr. Ruopp left five

dollars with that shopkeeper and said: "Whenever you hear of a poor child who can't buy marbles, I want you to give him some with my compliments."

Months later Dr. Ruopp got a letter from his paralytic friend informing him that that simple, kindly deed had transformed the town. The news of that act had spread like wildfire. "It was like a religious revival in our town, and no child or adult escaped its influence. 'So shines a good deed in a naughty world.' "

❖❖❖

"DAD, THEY MUST BELIEVE IT!"

IN a certain American city there lived a man and his wife who had three sons, all of them in the service of the nation.

Within two weeks there came three little government slips, indicating that each of those boys had been killed in action or was missing. It was a terrible blow to come to a single family, but that Christian family stood up under it like—well, like Christians.

It was close to Easter, and there was a good deal of friendly speculation and tender gossip all over the neighborhood the week preceding Easter as to whether those parents would be in their regular place on Sunday morning.

When Easter morning came they appeared in church as usual, walked silently with grief-stricken faces to their regular family pew. Grief-stricken faces, did I say? Yes, but with looks of almost an unearthly victory, poise, and calmness on their countenances also. It was an Easter sermon in itself, their very presence that morning. As the preacher looked at them when they seated themselves, he had a feeling that his Easter sermon had already been preached, that the spirit of the Easter victory was already in that pew and in that church. He remembered a phrase which his own children were using and smiled as he remembered it. It was

74

"out of this world." That described the look on the faces of those two parents. He smiled at them and they smiled back. It was like a benediction. He felt that in those faces he could actually see the Resurrection and their hope of immortality.

However, it remained for a small boy in the congregation to say the ultimate word which summed up that beautiful and dramatic experience. He was sitting in the pew immediately behind the father and mother. Naturally he had heard all the town gossip, speculation and wonder about whether that family would come to church on Easter morning. He kept his eye on them every minute of that solemn service. He saw them open their hymnbooks, rise and sing with the rest of the congregation. He saw them bow their heads reverently when the pastor prayed. He saw that they were listening intently and responding fervently to the responsive Bible reading of the morning, which was a victorious, triumphant reading about Christ having risen from the dead to redeem all human life from death. His small face looked puzzled. Then came the collection, and as it passed those parents, his keen eyes saw that the father, whom he knew to be a comparatively poor man, put a crisp new ten-dollar bill on the plate, as if he had not already given more than his share in giving his sons. It was more than the boy's curiosity could stand in one morning, and he pulled his father who sat beside him down to him and whispered with awe and boyish reverence into his father's ear: "Dad, they must believe it!"

The father, not catching clearly that small boy's whispered word, asked: "What do you mean, son?"

"Why, they must actually believe in Easter. They're here; they sang, they read the Bible, and what's more, they gave. Gosh—ten dollars. Dad, they must believe in Easter!"

❖❖❖

THE FIRES OF THE FATHERS

I WAS down in the TVA country one summer and heard this glorious tale.

It seems that the TVA was putting a deep lake in a certain valley and they had to condemn the land in that valley and move all the old-time settlers out. There were several mountain cabins on the sides of the slopes above that valley which was to be covered with water in due time. One of them had been owned by an old mountaineer for forty years.

When the government engineers went to see him about moving, he refused to move, even though the government offered him five times as much as his land and cabin were worth.

Then they built for him a stone house on the mountainside, not far away, with all modern conveniences, took him to the new house, and said: "Uncle Henry, this is all yours—a stone cabin, plastered rooms, a bath, a nice kitchen, with an electric stove and electric lights."

"Nope. Don't want it! Won't move!" replied the old man.

"Why not, Uncle Henry?"

"Gotta keep that fire goin' in the front room! My great-great-grandpap kept it goin'! My pappy kept it goin'! And I'm a goin' to keep it goin' too—I am! Can't let my pappy's fire go out, nohow!"

Then the group of government engineers, with typical American imagination, got a truck, gathered up the embers of the ancient fire and transported it with Uncle Henry to the new house on the hilltop overlooking the lake to be, and said to him: "There's your fire, Uncle Henry. We won't let it go out, and you can keep it burning up here as well as down in the valley."

Uncle Henry saw the logic of this arrangement and

76

agreed to accept the new home, now that the fires of his fathers were burning on the new hearth. He wanted to keep the fires of his fathers burning faithfully and perpetually and we can't blame the old mountaineer.

Fortunately the government had engineers with imagination and some respect for the traditional sentiments of the old mountaineer. Indeed most of us in this nation would be better off if we too had more reverence for the fires of our fathers—the fires of faith, the fires of freedom, the fires of religion, our dependence on God, our sense of integrity, loyalty, and democracy.

And we of the church would be better Christians, better men, happier in our business, homes, and human relationships if we too kept the fires of our Christian fathers burning on the altars of the church. And certainly one of those fires is the spirit of traditional Hebrew laws and the spirit of Christ and the New Testament.

Those were the fires of our early Christian fathers. Let us, in accepting the standards of Christian stewardship, tithing and sharing, keep the fires of our fathers burning on the altars of the church. At least let us be as faithful to our traditional religious past as that old mountaineer Uncle Henry.

❖❖❖

"CALAMITY JANE"

ONE of my books of short stories reached a friend in Australia, and he wrote me about it, enclosing a glowing story of his own. I believe it fits into the summer psychology of golfers who may read these lines, as well as into the meaning of our everyday life.

Strolling through a garden and around a house in the country, two men were companionably chatting and looking around. They strolled into an old shed at the end of the

77

yard. It was a storage place for old tools, garden equipment, some furniture, and a lot of miscellaneous odds and ends that had been discarded.

Giving a casual glance around the debris and castoffs, one of the men spied something of interest on a shelf and said: "What's that on the shelf, pal?"

Replied the other: "Just an old golf club." Then he took down an old rusty putter. The other man swung it in his hands, getting the feel of it in his sensitive firm fingers. He swung it over his head and said: "I like the feel of this. Mind if I keep it? You've evidently discarded it, for it is all rusty!"

"Take it away," said his friend. "I threw it on the shelf there several years ago and had completely forgotten it until you called it to my attention. And even when you discovered it there I wasn't greatly pleased, for the club had brought me nothing but calamity. I named it 'Calamity Jane.' Several years ago I had a particularly bad day in my putting, and it was that club which gave me my bad luck. So I consigned it to the pile of castoffs when I returned home after losing my game that afternoon. It's probably been there for two or three years, forgotten and unmourned. It's no good. If you want it, take it, and it's good riddance as far as I am concerned. Don't blame me if you lose your games trying to putt with that old iron."

Shortly after that conversation one of the most famous putts in golf was made with that putter. It was made on the eighteenth green at St. Andrews, for with it Bobby Jones won the open championship of Great Britain. He also won the U. S. national open championship the same year, the first player to win the two championships in the same year. Bobby Jones did this with the old discarded putter "Calamity Jane."

❖❖❖

"WHY DON'T YOU DO SOMETHING YOU CAN DO?"

THIS is the story of a successful man—now the president of a railroad—and his first job.

A lad in grammar school, he got a summer job as a section hand on a small Western railroad. He knew nothing about the work, was inexperienced, while all of the laborers of the section gang were seasoned hands, veterans of years of hard experience. The foreman gave the lad his first job, driving spikes into a tie. He hated to admit that he didn't know how to drive a spike, so when the foreman asked him if he did know how, he said he did.

The first spike got a quick jab with the heavy hammer when he put the spike in the tie, and then he swung that heavy hammer over his shoulder for the first real whack from a standing position. The hammer hit the spike a glancing blow and sent it about twenty feet away into a ditch which ran parallel with the roadbed. With a very reddened countenance he scrambled down into the ditch, hunted around for the spike, found it, and tried the trick again. This time he struck it a glancing blow and knocked it into the dich on the opposite side of the roadbed. Chagrined, he dropped his heavy hammer, searched for the spike and tried a third time. He missed it entirely, and looking up he saw that the foreman had been watching all three tries and was walking toward him with a stern expression on his face. He was ashamed and confused, but wholly unprepared for the remark that was whispered by the foreman confidentially: "Sonny, why don't you do something you can do?"

He was grateful to the foreman who did not let him down before the other men, and asked in a wistful manner if there was something else that he could do. The foreman asked him to help four of the other men carry ties and place them, and that he did well, for his young body was strong and sturdy.

After an interval of forty years my friend, now the president of that railroad, is still grateful to that kindly, understanding foreman who suggested that he do something he could do. And that little story points an arrow to the direction we can all take: A man can get as far in life by refusing to do those things which he knows he cannot do well, as by doing things he knows he can do!

ANCHORED TO SOMETHING WORTH WHILE

A FRIEND of mine is a great preacher and a great fisherman. He likes to take a week off now and then and go to a lake in Michigan and fish.

One day he noticed a group of fishermen at the northern end of the lake who were rapidly baiting and pulling in the perch, while he, at the other end of the lake, was not getting even a nibble. He decided to row his boat over to the little cove where they seemed to be having such good luck, and anchor to a tree stump he saw in the lake.

For a full hour he sat there fishing, and while the other fishermen about two hundred yards away were still getting bites, he was still getting nothing at all. As the afternoon wore on he suddenly realized that he was farther and farther away from the other group.

Investigating, he discovered that he had anchored his boat not to a tree stump, as he thought, but to a floating log which looked like a tree stump jutting out of the water. He chuckled to himself as the saw what he had done, and said, preacherlike; "If a dumb guy anchors his boat to a

80

floating log he must expect to drift with the currents; if he wants to anchor his boat or his life to something, why doesn't he have sense enough to anchor it to something that is stable and permanent, like the church, or home, a community, or to religion."

He said to me: "I saw at once that I could go to town with an experience and a story like that, so I was glad that I had not caught any fish that day. I had caught a great illustration and I had caught a great idea. Since that day I have been using it as a subject in my talks to young people, and older people too. I've been telling them that if they want to anchor their lives to something, investigate to ascertain if it's worth while—like the church, the Bible or religion, good character, honest friends, a college education, or what have you. For the love of Mike, and good sense, anchor yourself to something worth while and permanent!"

The vernacular in which the story was told was amusing to me. A more cultured, refined minister than either of us could "go to town" with that idea even though he put it in the language of the fisherman and the parlance of the every-day man.

❖❖❖

"PET THE CALF AND CATCH THE COW"

IN one of my talks before a group of ministers in a Texas community, endeavoring to help them in the affairs of the church. I used several little stories to show them how to increase attendance, persuade men to become members, and generally arouse the enthusiasm of the general community to the church idea.

One story was about the young ensign who came to see me in Boston because he remembered me from twenty years before when I had given him a package of Life Savers. Then I told them the story of Dr. Dillon Bronson, a great Methodist minister who carried around in his pocket, small deflated rubber toy balloons to hand out to the little ones in his church, and how he was remembered by my daughter Betty, not as a preacher but as the man who gave her several balloons when she was a little girl.

I was so interesed in my subject that I seemed to forget that I was talking to ministers who lived in a cow country, and when we came to an open forum discussion of the matter of winning adults to the church by first serving and loving their children, a big, raw-boned, sun-tanned minister, who looked very like a cow hand himself, arose and said: "Dr. Stidger, I've lived in this cow country all my days. I have preached in this man's land for thirty years and most of my churches have been rural churches. I like what you told us this morning about how to enlist the parents in church work through looking after and loving their children and the young people. Maybe you'd like to know one of our Texas sayings that puts into a single phrase all the things you've talked about to us this morning."

"I'd certainly like to hear that phrase, my friend. Shoot!" The word "shoot" was not used simply because it originated in Texas, for I have been saying "shoot" all my days in such a situation.

"Down here in Texas we say: 'Pet the calf and catch the cow!' How's that for saying what you want to say, Doctor?"

"I'll say it is O.K., pal! And I sincerely thank you for handing it on to me in this connection. I'm going to school to you this morning, and I'll be using that phrase, 'Pet the calf and catch the cow!' all my days hereafter."

❖❖❖

"HOW'S YOUR BACK THESE DAYS?"

I LIKE to talk with the men who shine my shoes. I hate to waste time just sitting, doing nothing while the polishing is being done. Every human being has a story in him if you can get him to talk.

In the Albany, New York, railroad station I was getting my shine from a middle-aged Italian, bright-eyed and friendly. He straightened from his stooping position with his paste and rag, and I noticed that he winced.

It was a hot, murky morning. He didn't seem inclined to talk, for he replied to my comments in grunts and mono-sylables, and didn't open up a bit. I am no reporter to accept a turndown like that without using some of an interviewer's tricks. Having noticed that he winced when he stood up, I said to him: "How's your back these days?"

Instantly he looked up, felt of his back, smiled a broad, friendly smile beneath his gray walrus-like mustache, and gave me the story of his lame back, what the hospitals had done for and to him for months. He talked volubly like a spring torrent from that question on. All it took to prime the reluctant pump of his personality was that universal question: "How's your back these days?" It's a universal sesame for people who have reached middle age!

The first time I interviewed Cyrus Dallin, the famous sculptor, he was not a bit interested. It was no treat to that great man, just as legs were no treat to the London bus driver. I couldn't get that fine old man to talk. He was plainly bored with me, my presence, and my questions. I finally reached his heart when I asked: "Mr. Rallin, tell me about your mother."

Instantly his face lighted up, he laughed aloud and said: "Now we're getting some place. When I get to talking about my dear old mother I'm just a silly old goose." From that minute on we had a glorious time. For a whole hour he reminisced about his mother—and for me the sailing was good. I had primed the pump of his personality and his memory with that simple question. It taught me a lesson in

83

interviewing—If you want to get your story, ask a man about his mother, his children, his father, his old boyhood home—or ask: "How's your back these days?"

❖❖❖

"SURE 'NUF FREN'S!"

A SOUTHERN woman I have known for many years has a Negro girl who does the family washing. She thoroughly enjoyed watching the girl hanging out her washing, and leaning over the fence laughing and chatting hilariously with the Negro girl in the neighboring house who was also in the process of hanging out the family washing. It seemed that they always managed to be hanging out their washing at the same hour each morning, and they talked and laughed so uproariously that the whole neighborhood could hear them.

The two white women who were neighbors thought that it was a fine thing that the two girls could be such pals. Then one morning Mrs. Johnson noticed that as the girls hung out their washings there was no chatting, no laughter. She was puzzled at her Maggie's cool relationship with her friend and spoke to her when she came into the house: "I noticed that you and Mary aren't talking and laughing this morning, Maggie. What's the trouble, have you quarrelled about something?"

"No, ma'am, we ain't quarrelled; we jes' ain't speakin' no more!"

"Why, Maggie, I'm surprised, I thought that you and Mary were bosom friends."

"No, ma'am, Mary and me ain't no sure 'nuf, regular bosom fren's like you say; we has jest laffed together; we ain't cried together none."

And whether the girl knew it or not, she was expressing a profound psychological truth in human relationships.

84

Maggie had probably never heard of Kahlil Gibran, the Syrian poet, author of the best-selling *Prophet,* but a few years ago he said exactly what Maggie said: "You can forget those with whom you have laughed, but you can never forget those with whom you have wept."

There is universal truth in these two statements, one from the simple girl and the other from a profound prophet and poet. In these present days, when people are sorrowing for their lost loved ones in the aftermath of a war, it is good to know and remember that weeping together binds people to each other with hoops of steel forever.

❖❖❖

WORTHY OF HIS HIRE

IN these days of strikes and work stoppages it is not untimely to read of an experience of the great steel industrialist Charles M. Schwab. He himself writes it:

I happened to be walking through one of our plants and stopped to talk to one of the men who has been working for us a long time. He shoveled ore.

"How much do you get a week?" I asked him.

He told me.

"You ought to be getting more than that!" I said to him. "We ought to pay you a certain amount extra after you have shoveled a stated amount each day."

"There would be no use in doing that," he answered, "because I work as hard as I can, and no matter how hard I work I can't shovel more than a ton of ore in a day."

However, I made the arrangements so that the chap should be paid more if he shoveled more.

A few weeks later I happened to run into him again. He looked abashed and embarrassed. "What's the matter, Flynn?" I queried.

He stammered and halted in his response and then said, "I'll tell you, Mr. Schwab. The last time I saw you I told you I couldn't shovel more than a ton of ore a day. I thought I was telling you the truth at that time. But since you have made the new arrangement I am handling four tons a day, and it does not seem as hard work as the one ton formerly did. Each time a shovelful shoots through the air I say to myself: 'There goes some more money for Flynn.' "

Let this story talk for itself in these days of industrial controversy, strikes, and stoppages. I believe it is something that both labor and management might ponder with profit, and over which we of the purchasing public might also ponder for a few moments as we condone or condemn labor and capital. Industrial reality confronts all of us in these days of uncertainty, and I wish that every laborer, industrialist, and representative in Washington might read this story and take it to heart.

THAT STOCKYARD JUDAS

I RECEIVED a clipping from a Chicago newspaper, sent by a friend of mine, which told about a tragedy in the stockyards of that great city.

For many years they had a goat called "Judas," who was trained to lead the millions of lambs to the slaughter in the stockyards. He had been trained to lead a thousand lambs down an incline, and when he came to a certain spot on the incline he jumped quickly aside into another runway but the poor lambs behind him were quickly jerked up on a piece of machinery and their throats cut. However, on a certain day Brother Judas, being an old goat and absent-minded, forgot to turn at the right spot into the safe runway and was himself suddenly jerked to his death and his own throat was cut—just as Napoleon and Hitler and a lot of Judases in human history have had their throats cut in the long run. It invariably ends that way.

Edwin Markham expressed it in a quatrain which he calls "Even Scales."

> The robber is robbed by his riches,
>   The tyrant is dragged by his chain;
> The schemer is snared by his cunning;
>   The slayer lies dead by the slain.

I have always refused to be discouraged or dismayed by the apparent ascendency of a Dillinger, a Huey Long, small-town or home-tyrant, a Mussolini, a Hitler, or a Franco, or a student who will not study but who slides through school. Time will take care of all of them in the spirit of this verse:

> Though the mills of God grind slowly,
>   Yet they grind exceedingly small.
>   .   .   .   .
> And when they went to look for Brother Judas,
>   He wasn't there—at all, at all!

The last two lines are mine—not so smooth but with as much meaning. The "Judas" who is unfaithful to his home and family, the small-town capitalist who exploits the poor of the town, the mean citizen, verily "they have their reward," for "the soul that sinneth, it shall die" is eternally true.

In a great book of fiction called *The Herdsman,* by Dorothy Clarke Wilson, is this observation on life: "There's something about meanness, I've noticed, that sort of punishes itself, if you wait long enough. It is in the very nature of things."

❖❖❖

"IT'S A MAJOR PLANET TO US!"

A FAMOUS scientist was talking with a friend of mine about the atomic bomb, and my friend, determined to pump the scientist dry of all information asked: "Doctor, I want to know all that you know about this atomic bomb. Now just what would have happened if they had used a bomb ten times as large as the bomb they did use, and had allowed it to explode above the water in the air?"

"Well," answered the scientist, carefully and slowly, "it is conceivable that the power could have consumed all the nitrogen in the air and burned the world to a crisp.

"And what might have happened if they had exploded such a large bomb under the water?"

"Well," replied the scientist, discreetly, "it is conceivable that it might have united with the oxygen in the sea and consumed all the water and blown up the earth."

"That would mean the annihilation of the earth, wouldn't it?"

"Yes," he replied, cautiously but deliberately, "but, after all, our earth is not one of the major planets.

"That may be," replied my friend, "but it's a major planet to us!"

That story reminded me of one about a wedding ceremony that I was about to officiate at when the mother in the home said to me: "Doctor, you may have performed a thousand weddings but remember that this is our first wedding." I knew what she meant.

Hearing one of those smart boys in a group who was holding forth to prove that World War II was not such a bad war after all, that more people were killed in factories, automobile accidents, and civilian life than in battle, I noted a quiet little man interrupted him just as he reached the point of all-out eloquence, to say: "That may all be true

88

but to my family it was a pretty terrible war for our boy was killed in the Battle of the Bulge." That took the wind out of the sails of our friend who was trying to prove that it was just a mild war after all, and it deflated the boy's argument and eloquence ultimately and completely. He became silent.

No theory will change the very human fact that it is what hits each one of us personally that counts in this life. When trouble, war, death, or atomic bombs hit us personally then it means something to us personally, and it is in that mood that we must be looking at the hunger of the rest of the world, the loneliness of displaced persons, the tragedy of Palestine and its people, disastrous fires that take so many lives, flooded areas that wipe out towns and take a toll of humanity, and the everyday tragedies that strike the great number of people all over the world.

❖❖❖

A BUMBLEBEE ATTITUDE

I THOROUGHLY enjoyed speaking before a school of Negro preachers at Gammon Theological Seminary one summer. Preceding every class they sang Negro spirituals for me, and as only Negroes know how to sing the spirituals. The dean said to me: "What I have to do in this school is to make these boys want to learn, to read, to search for material. They don't know how to do that or why they should do it."

Reaching around for a figure of speech which would do that very thing occupied my time in addition to lecturing about it every day. One hot evening in June I was sitting on the front steps of the Recitation Hall at Gammon waiting for my class to appear when I saw a big bumblebee whirring and hovering over a honeysuckle bush. It was twilight; evidently the busy bumblebee was alone and the other bees in their hives or hideaways. In spite of all the rules that his union might have had, that bee was working overtime seeking honey. He would hover eagerly over a flower, jump to another flower, to another and another. He would poke his head, in fact his whole body, down into a flower and suck all the honey out. His body and legs and wings were covered with pollen. He dipped, I should say he zoomed, into more than one hundred flowers in a few minutes for I counted. I never saw a more eager hunter after honey than that bumblebee. It was an inspiration to watch him.

That evening I told my class about the bumblebee and how he plunged into every flower on that bush, how he worked long after bee union hours, when all the other bees had hived up. I told the students that the bee could show a preacher how he ought to work—plunging into the flower of every book, every experience, every human interest story, every classroom, every book of the immortal Bible, every little child's experience, every adult's experience, and every adventure that life offers him. A preacher, like the bumblebee, ought to work overtime; work while other bees are hived up, work after union hours to get the honey of the experiences of life.

❖❖❖

HE ALMOST TOLD HER

WHEN I was a student preacher in a Cape Cod town I lived with a typical New England couple. They were the most inarticulate couple I ever knew. I never heard either of them express a kind or an appreciative word to the other. And yet I had the feeling that they loved and respected each other deeply.

One Saturday morning the woman died, and it was my task to comfort the old New England sea captain. I sat with him for hours. I mentioned that the woman was the best cook I had ever known, that she cooked the best baked beans

I had ever tasted. He nodded his head and agreed with me. I mentioned that she was the most kindly person I had ever known, and called his attention to the fact that when anybody in the little Cape Cod town was ill or in distress he always sent for Aunt Martha to see him through his trouble. He nodded his head in agreement.

Then I mentioned that for her age she was certainly a neat, clean woman, and, in a sun and windburned way, she had a certain stately beauty about her walk and her personal appearance, a beauty that many a younger woman might envy. He agreed to that also.

I felt it incumbent upon me, being a minister, to mention her character and her religious life, and of how much she meant to the church, that we could never have gotten along without her. I spoke of her faithfulness and loyalty to the preacher, the services, and the church, of her generous giving of her money and her time to the church. He nodded again in agreement with me.

After two hours of talking the old Cape Codder looked at me and frankly admitted that he loved his deceased wife, and as he finally got it out: "So much so that there were certain times when I come near tellin' her about it."

That experience was a good lesson, for the very tragedy of that wistful statement made me resolve that when I had a kindly impulse to say a good word to somebody, to tell somebody close to me of my love, to write a friendly letter when I felt that someone deserved it, I would do it without delay. So I learned something from that old Cape Codder.

A BIG GAME HUNTER

JACKIE, aged four, came running into my room, wild-eyed with excitement, and yelled at me, "Da! [that's short for grandfather] there's a line, tiger, helephunt, bear, and a rinoserush down in the 'veen [that's short for ravine]. Let's kill 'em!"

Who was I to permit a menagerie of wild beasts like that to loaf around in our ravine menacing the security and the playground of my grandson? Only a coward would stand by and permit that to happen. So up I jumped, grabbed a wooden gun and loaded it; and Jackie and I started down into the ravine for some wild game hunting. On the way down I was expecting every minute that Jackie would renege, try to explain away those ferocious animals as imaginary animals. But not Jackie. He was very serious about it. The animals that he saw menacing his life were very real in his little mind. When he gave his commands for us to get down and crawl on our bellies to surprise them, and to remove my shoes when I awkwardly stepped on a twig and made a noise, I followed them. We must surprise those wild animals and kill every one of them. I crept on my fat tummy under low-hanging trees, wondering every minute how far Jackie would carry this farce.

Finally we got to the bottom of the ravine, and Jackie stopped me behind a bush and pointed out the exact locations of the "line," the tiger, the "helephunt," and the bear. I wondered how he would get out of this dilemma and what explanation he would make when no wild animals actually appeared. Suddenly there was a noise in the trees and I heard the yelp of Gerta, our little flat dachshund. She was chasing a squirrel. Then Jackie exploded: "There! They's running away 'cause they knowed my Da would shoot 'em! They know when to run 'way when a big game hunter comes 'round!"

I had been telling yarns to little Jackie about the times that I was a big game hunter in the West Virginia hills. That was through the sheer necessity of story telling and had little fact in it. I was beginning to wonder if I had made a liar out of Jackie when suddenly I remembered an ancient Chinese proverb: "Imagination is greatness on the way," and that let us both out of a tight situation!

❖❖❖

RAINY DAY PHILOSOPHY

IN AN Ohio town around five o'clock in the morning, a sudden downpour of terrific rain came like a cloudburst. A young mother said to her husband: "Hurry downstairs and pull down the screens on the porch or the porch furniture will be soaked!"

The sleepy young father jumped out of bed, hurried downstairs, and let down the porch screens. When he returned from that emergency task, there on the step that led from the living room to the porch sat his pajama-clad five-year-old son, a big grin on his face. He too had been awakened by the downpour and, seeking adventure, had followed his father downstairs. They sat together on the stoop, and the father put his arms around his son and watched the rain pouring down. The morning was depressing and very gloomy and the father was silent thinking what havoc the rain was to cause for their work and how it would shatter their picnic plans for that Saturday.

Then his five-year-old son looked up at him with a twinkle in his blue eyes and said: "It's a gorgeous bad day, isn't it, Daddy?"

The father let out a whoop, picked Billy up in his arms, and carried him upstairs laughing all the way. When he told his wife the reason for his laughter, she too started to laugh. Jackie in the next room asked what his parents were laughing about, and when they told him that Billy had said, "It's a gorgeous bad day," Jackie joined in the laughter and the whole family was convulsed with laughter. Billy was right. It was a "gorgeous bad day," for Billy had, without

knowing it, sensed what a poet said long ago about just
such a morning:

> It is not raining rain to me,
> It's raining daffodils.

There is actually such a thing as "a gorgeous bad day" to
one who has imagination. Some of the most beautiful days
I have ever experienced have been rainy, dark days when
every leaf seemed to be washed a cleaner green and shone
in the darkness, when every rhododendron seemed to be a
cleaner pink, purple, and brilliant red, when every blade
of grass seemed to have been washed clean of all its dirt,
when even a child seemed to sense that

> It is not raining rain to me,
> It's raining violets.

❖❖❖

SUN DIALS SAY THINGS

YES, I like sundials. I like to read the inscriptions on them.
I have a collection of such inscriptions.

One of the best I know is an inscription once found by
Alexander Woollcott on a dial: "It is later than you think,
friend!"

Another that I like is: "I record only the sunny hours."

On the day that President Franklin D. Roosevelt passed
away I happened to be crossing Harvard Yard. I had crossed
it a thousand times before, but I had never stopped to read
the inscription on the sundial in the Yard. That day I was
in a thoughtful mood and stopped to read it. Here it is:
"On this minute hangs eternity."

How dramatically that inscription burned itself into the
meaning of that dire day. I stood there remembering that

President Roosevelt, as a college student, had passed by that dial hundreds of times, that he had walked under those rapidly greening trees in the old Yard, and that he too had often stood in the shadow of those ancient buildings.

Then, as I stood there, that inscription brought back to my memory a saying of Thomas Carlyle which began to ring in my heart like the toll of the president's funeral bells: "Man? Stands he not at the center of immensities: at the conflux of eternities?"

I looked up into the sky and had a sudden feeling that I, as an individual, was actually standing at that minute in the very center of immensity; that, at that very minute, I was actually standing at the "conflux of eternities"; that all the time there ever was, was behind me, and that all the time and eternity there would ever be was before me; that that very minute, that very second, was the heart of time and the universe. Then I suddenly knew the full meaning of all immensities and all time: "On this minute hangs eternity!"

What a simple statement was inscribed on that sun dial, and what a wallop there was in the inscription: a sudden awareness of the value of time; that no minutes, no seconds, are to be idly wasted; that every second is like so much precious gold, to be used and lived and laughed in and loved in; that every minute of time and eternity are invaluable.

❖❖❖

"BE IT EVER SO JUMBLED, THERE'S NO PLACE LIKE HOME"

A WOMAN friend of mine who travels constantly saw in the newspapers that a department store in Chicago had several thousand nylons for sale one morning. She needed nylons (what woman doesn't?) and had some time to spare, so she went over to see what would happen. Well, plenty happened. She is a little, short woman and found herself in the midst of a mob of women, all shoving, pushing, biting, and battling females. Before she got anywhere near the nylon counter her dress was half torn off, she had two long scratches down her face, and she had lost a valuable pin, and one earring.

Not only that, but she had engaged in two verbal battles with belligerent women, one of whom bawled at her in language that would have made a truck driver blush with shame. She came away from the encounter ashamed for herself, her sex, and the human race, saying: "No wonder we cannot achieve world peace if women in a civilized nation will scratch, yell, shove, and curse each other over a few pair of nylons."

She caught a train to Boston, and when she arrived she got in a taxicab, still smarting under the experience in Chicago, and still very much disgusted with humanity. However, the driver brought back her faith in human beings, for as they drove through the streets to her home this is what she discovered about the man:

There were sixteen people living in his five-room-house; that his brother and his family, and his wife's sister and her family, and his mother-in-law were all living with them, due to the badly congested housing problems.

"That must be awful!" Mrs. LeSourd sympathized with the taxi driver.

"Oh, no! It isn't half bad. We have a lot of fun together. We share the expenses of living, the women share the work, we go to movies—and we get a big kick out of it! In fact I can hardly wait to get home each evening when I am through my work. I even love my mother-in-law. We are good pals, and she is a lot of fun. She takes my part in an argument. I'm strong for my mother-in-law!"

"Well, you redeem the human race for me, and I certainly needed something like this to bring back my faith in humanity," said Mrs. LeSourd. She related her Chicago experience, and they had a good laugh together over that, especially when she showed him her facial scratches from the "Battle of the Nylons."

"Well, it's like this, lady. Be it ever so jumbled, there's no place like home!"

Mrs. LeSourd had a good laugh and replied, "You're right—no matter how jumbled, there's no place like home, and that says it exactly. Noise and confusion, even discomfort—there's no place like home!"

"I'll say there ain't!" agreed the cab driver.

And I believe that my friend came out of that experience with a new faith in humanity, the American citizen, and the American home, with a new faith that perhaps after all we may work out a settled world and see peace "at long last."

A NEW DEFINITION OF "INFINITESIMAL"

ONE day I read this bit of dialogue which gave me a chuckle:

Teacher: "Give me a definition of the word 'infinitesimal.'"

Student: "Infinitesimal is that interval of time which elapses between the time the green light goes on in front of you and the time the automobile back of you toots its horn for you to move along."

That definition of the word "infinitesimal" gave me a laugh because I have been both the victim and the culprit in that little everyday drama of American life. It seems instinctive to feel that the man in front of you is sound

97

asleep at his wheel when the light turns green, and you usually have an impulse to, and usually do, toot your horn to awaken him from his lethargy. You yourself when you are the victim of that tooting usually speak your little word about his brainlessness and what you usually say is: "Whassa matta with that guy behind me, is he going to a fire or something? Whassa hurry, nut?"

The philosophy of driving needs attention in this nation. We all have the spirit of dictatorship; we are all unreasonable tyrants when we are at the wheel of an automobile and we act as if we own the highway and as if every other driver were a dumb guy. Driving an automobile, we turn into Hitlers and Mussolinis.

A friend of mine was driving along when someone was going too slowly for him so he muttered to himself: "That fool, why is he driving so slowly?"

A little later another car cut in on him because that car wanted to go ahead and thought that my friend was driving too slowly. My friend yelled after him: "That fool, is he going to a fire or something?"

A third driver started up too slowly to suit my friend when the green light came on, and once again he muttered into his beard: "That fool, is he asleep at the wheel?"

His five-year-old daughter Jane had been calmly sitting in the back seat listening to her father's outbursts against every driver on the highway. She suddenly echoed her father's complaints in this startling and vehement phrase in the same indignant tones of her father: "One big fool! Two big fools! Three big fools! Hey, Dad, they're all big fools, aren't they?"

Much to the chagrin of her father, Janie had caught the spirit of her father's indignation, and much to the hilarious delight of her mother, who was sitting beside her husband and was not entirely enjoying his exclamations of impatience and his implied criticism of every driver but himself until his little girl spoke her piece.

There is a chuckle in this story, but there is also a serious note which is intended for all of us, for we Americans are becoming the most intolerant people on earth when it comes to our traffic attitudes and manners. Everyone is wrong—but us! Our impatience is foolish and our language directed against our fellow man in traffic is something we would not use in polite society. We would be insulted if someone called us a lot of Hitlers and Mussolinis but that is our attitude in traffic. We are right and everybody else is wrong and ought to get out of our way—and quickly.

"OUT OF WHAT YOU HAVE IN LIFE, MAKE MUSIC, MY FRIEND!"

I WAS watching the Cleveland American League team play the Boston Red Sox and witnessed one of the most dramatic, spectacular catches I have ever seen. Cleveland's right fielder ran halfway across the field, the bright sun shining directly into his eyes, reached his left hand and arm over into the bleachers so far that he hurt his side, and grabbed a foul out of the air, held it high above his head and then fell to the ground. It was terribly exciting, but even that is not all the story.

Three innings later the man was back in the game and was running for another fly when he fell to the ground, got up, staggered around and yelled for the second baseman to come to his aid. The game was stopped by the umpire, and the club trainer came running out into right field with his little first-aid kit. The fielder was led off the field to the dressing room. As he went down the dugout steps we noticed that he groped and felt his way like a blind man.

He was a blind man, for he only had one good eye to begin with, and suddenly that afternoon his other eye lost its sight. Earlier in the season he had been hit squarely in the left eye by a batted ball, and the eye went stone blind. However, he had been playing all the rest of the season with sight in only one eye, and then that had given out. The point of the story is that he used what he had and played with the sight of one eye—and in the field at that. Also, he seldom made an error and he caught every ball that came his way; that last desperate catch with his left arm extended over the bleachers being an illustration of what he could do.

An inspiring story is also told of the player with the Washington Senators who has two wooden legs—and he plays a fine game. There is a one-armed man playing for the St. Louis Browns who can field and bat with the skill of a man having two arms, and he is a constant inspiration to thousands of returned soldiers who lost arms and legs and eyes in the war. If the ball clubs are giving us these players intentionally it is a wonderful thing, but I have never found out.

Robert Browning, in one of his fine poems, urges the human race to do the best it can with what it has. Here is part of that poem:

> The common problem, yours, mine, every one's,
> Is—not to fancy what were fair in life
> Provided it could be, but, finding first
> What may be, then find how to make it fair
> Up to our means: a very different thing!
> My business is not to remake myself,
> But make the absolute best of what God made!

Long ago another poet put it this way: "Out of what you have in life, make music, friend!"

There never was a time when that gospel was more pertinent than in these days when we have so many wounded men to rehabilitate, and whose rehabilitation, in the final analysis, is in their own hands, or when we have so much of a world to rebuild. All we can do is to try and catch the spirit of "Out of what you have in life, make music, friend!"

❖❖❖

"NOTHING IS JUST ORDINARY"

SEVERAL years ago I was talking with Ralph Adams Cram, the American famous architect who designed and built the West Point Chapel, the university chapel at Princeton, the Cathedral of St. John the Divine in New York, the Cathedral of SS. Peter and Paul in Washington, and hundreds of other great Gothic projects in this nation.

In his beautiful home near Boston he told me a story of William Walcot, the English etcher, who came to New York in the early twenties to sketch New York skyscrapers.

For several weeks he simply wandered around the great city gathering impressions of those high mountainous buildings, and he was deeply impressed. To Mr. Cram he said: "Here in this country you have developed an entirely new architecture which fits the great expanses of your land. It is indigenous. It is what you call stupendous and it fits into your American mood and spirit. It seems that you do things in a big way here."

Then one morning he suddenly felt in the mood to record some of his impressions. He tried in vain to obtain sketching paper, but it was Sunday and all the art stores were closed and he could not find what he wanted. He remembered that Mr. Cram often worked in his office on Sunday mornings, and at that time he was giving much of his time to the plans for St. John the Divine.

However, he did not find Mr. Cram in his office that

Sunday, but an office boy was there wrapping up house plans, and Walcot asked: "What is that paper, boy?"

"Oh, just ordinary wrapping paper," replied the boy.

"Nothing is just ordinary," corrected the artist, "if you know how to use it. Give me some of that ordinary paper, as you call it, and I'll show you what I mean when I say that nothing is ordinary."

With a master's touch Mr. Walcot executed two sky-scraper sketches. One later sold for a thousand dollars, and the other for five hundred dollars. They are now master-pieces which will live among the most famous etchings of the world.

We used to see certain unimpressive, pimply-faced youths jerking sodas in our corner drugstores, boys who were so ordinary that we would not give them a second look on our village streets. Those same boys were soon flying half-million-dollar bombers over Japan and wearing medals of courage and heroism.

World War II taught us that "nothing is just ordinary"; there were no ordinary boys, no ordinary times, no ordinary feelings. The nations and the people were not ordinary. And we have found that just ordinary people are full of courage, sacrifice, and heroism.

One day Quentin Roosevelt came running into the White House and told his father that he had been playing with some common little boys on the lawn. President Theodore Roosevelt replied, and Quentin never forgot the lesson: "Quentin, there are no common little boys. There are large and small boys, there are black and white boys, there are fat and slender boys, but there is no such thing as a common boy."

"Nothing is just ordinary!"

❖❖❖

"BUT YOU CALLED ME BROTHER!"

ALTHOUGH I thought that I had read everything that Tolstoy had ever written, I happened to miss the story that my friend Wesley Boyd, a Methodist minister, told me. This story is especially applicable to social conditions in a postwar period.

Tolstoy, who always had deep sympathy for the poor and gave away much that he owned, once passed a beggar on a village street in Russia during a war famine. The man was emaciated, starved almost to death, and, as usual, begging alms.

Tolstoy searched in his pockets for something to give to the beggar, for his generous heart went out in a sincere pity for the man, but he found no coin, because of the simple fact that all day long he had been giving away money.

However, he kissed him on each sunken cheek, took him into his arms, and said: "Do not be angry with me, my brother, I have nothing to give you."

The thin face of that beggar lighted with a great glow, became illuminated as if a great inner light had transformed it, and he whispered in reply, as the tears ran down his cheeks: "But you called me brother—that is a great gift!"

I was deeply moved by the story, for I had just read Richard Wright's *Black Boy*, one of the most discussed books of the year. It had been banned in many cities, and yet to me it is a great and useful social document. I had little opportunity to read it until it had been out for several months, but I finally got to its pages with a certain dread and eagerness, for some had said that it was a gruesome, cruel, and hard story. Others had said that it was a beautiful, tender, kindly, eager, hopeful story of what a Negro boy goes through in the South, at least an intelligent one.

I actually found it to be the story of a Negro boy who

103

went about this world with a great wistful eagerness to find someone, black or white, brown or yellow, who would walk up to him and call him "brother." It was his hope, his faith, his dream, his goal. And at long last he found such a man. Now Richard Wright is going on to glory in his creative self-expression.

Indeed, what most of us want is somebody, in the spirit of Tolstoy, to call us "brother." This poor, distracted world wants and needs a "brother." Human beings are human beings, and the hungers of one are the hungers of all. Nationality and color do not change the basic needs and the hungers of humanity. The whole world hungers for brotherhood, and brotherhood is the only thing which will cure the deep distress of the world.

❖❖❖

DON'T TURN YOUR BACK TO THE SEA!

I HAVE visited Atlantic City hundreds of times, but it seemed more fascinating than ever during the years of World War II, when the government was using all the magnificent hotels to reassign and rehabilitate the boys who returned from the war zones. The boys, with their wives and children, lived there for as long a time as was necessary, until they were well and strong. Their expenses were all paid, including the expenses of their families, and they had a glorious time strolling along the famous boardwalk, doing whatever they pleased. For many young soldiers it was a second honeymoon, for many of them their honeymoons following a wartime marriage.

I happened to be there a few weeks visiting with a chaplain friend who had been wounded in the last week of the European war and had been flown back to recuperate. Walking down the boardwalk he called my attention to the seats on the edge of the walk that were so placed that those who rested there had their eyes on the glittery, tinselly shops, with their souvenirs and shells and cheap gaudy articles for sale, and their backs to the great and beautiful ocean. In all the trips I had made to that resort I had never noticed that.

"They probably arranged those benches so that those who sit on them are forced to look at the cheap, tinsel-filled places. They were arranged in this way before the war because this was almost entirely a commercial enterprise," said my chaplain friend. Then he added: "But a lot of us soldiers have changed the seats and benches so that we can look out on the great expanse of sea rather than the commercial scenery. After all, whatever healing of the soul there is at this place is to be found in the sea. I believe that most of the soldiers prefer to look at the sea. I certainly do."

I humbly remarked: "I guess that is the way a good many of us live our lives. We turn our backs to the wonderful and beautiful things and keep our eyes on the transient and dross of life. We do not contemplate the sunsets, stars, sunrises; glow and glory of the eternal. We too often keep our eyes on the passing and ugly things of life. We seem to turn our backs on the cultural and spiritual things and face the fleeting and amusing incidents. I believe that certain radio comedians are heard by many, many more than listen to the Boston Symphony or the Metropolitan Opera broadcasts."

The chaplain replied: "Doctor, I want you to know that we, who have looked upon death constantly for the past few years, have turned about two thirds of those benches around so that they face the great ocean with its rolling billows, its glorious sunrises, and its world horizons. We are thinking in terms of internationalism, brotherhood, cleanliness, and beauty. We have seen death, and we are searching for the eternal things. We feast our eyes on beauty and a bigger world whenever we can."

I felt well repaid for my trip to Atlantic City by just talking to the young chaplain and to have that symbol of life called to my attention. I shall never turn my back to the beautiful and the eternal things to look on the trivial and passing that I shall not remind myself of the benches on the boardwalk at Atlantic City. They were turned to face the sea by the soldiers, that they might see wider horizons.

❖❖❖

"BEFORE YOU PASSED THIS WAY"

HENRY WARD BEECHER was a kindly, pleasant heart-warming man, in addition to being one of this nation's great and unforgettable preachers in his day. The famous Yale lectures were named in his honor and are still being given each year at Yale Divinity School. He still lives in many forms but perhaps lives longest of all because of his kindness and his love.

One cold, bitter morning the great man was walking down a street in New York, and he stopped to buy a newspaper from a shivering poorly clad boy. But Henry Ward Beecher, as usual, was not content just to buy a newspaper and to take no recognition of the fact that he was dealing with a human being. He had great respect for human personality, and every man, woman, and child was a distinctive individual to him. That is the mark of true greatness in any man—his reverence for personality as such. Beecher paid for his paper, which concluded his business deal with the newsboy, and then he stopped to talk with him for a minute and to inquire about his home, his goals, and his feelings. As he turned to leave the boy, he said out of the fullness of his heart: "Poor little fellow! Aren't you cold standing on this corner unprotected?"

Looking up at the big man, a radiant smile on his face, the boy replied: "I was, sir—before you passed this way."

Another story in like vein is the one told of John Wesley, who went through many English villages on his preaching tours. One day Cardinal Newman noticed that in certain villages in the coal-mining section the people were happy, the houses pretty with geraniums and other flowers outside the homes, the women dressed neatly. It was surprising because they lived in an atmosphere of coal dust. He asked a villager: "Why is it that this village is so clean and everything so well taken care of by the people? How do you account for it when other English villages are so dirty and the people so slovenly?"

The villager answered: "It is because several years ago a man named John Wesley passed through this village."

On the same theme we have a story about a modern John Wesley and Henry Ward Beecher. Dr. Fred Winslow Adams, who lived in Boston, passed away at the ripe old age of eighty. His passing was honored by many, many people, and still today we see signs of his having gone our way in the beautiful things that he left behind. One of those monuments to his memory is a great and beautiful Gothic church in Springfield, Massachusetts. It is called Trinity Church.

One day I was talking with a man who had been in that church, and he said to me: "I came to Springfield when a young man to work. I came from the country and was lonely and frightened. Dr. Adams took me into his home for the first week I was there and into his heart for all the remaining years of his life. Everything that Dr. Adams touched he made more beautiful, and the church is only a symbol of what he did for individual lives. Everything he touched he always made more beautiful."

Add to those stories the immortal story of Robert Louis Stevenson, who, as a sick boy, would watch the old Scot lamplighter come down his street in Edinburgh every evening at dusk to light the oil lamps. Later in life Stevenson said of that old lamplighter, as a symbol of all intellectual, spiritual, and friendly human beings: "This is what I remember of that lamplighter each evening: wherever he went he always left a light behind him."

❖❖❖

"AMONG THE FACES OF THE PASSERS-BY"

SOMETIME ago I ran across this verse in my old Scot mother's scrapbook. It certainly shows me how to get a lot more out of life:

> Give me not scenes more charming, give me eyes
> To see the beauty that around me lies;
> To read the trials of souls, see angels shy
> Among the faces of the passers-by.

The very same day I read that verse I also read a story which illustrates what the verse means. It happened in a church. Almost everybody had left the choirroom after a Sunday morning service except a small boy and the aged organist emeritus, who was ninety years old. He was trying hard to zip the zippers on his overshoes but was having a hard time.

The small boy, seeing his difficulty, bounded down from the chancel, stooped on one knee, and with a smile like the sunlight of all out of doors, zipped the overshoes of the old man, saying even as he was doing his good deed: "Mr. Booth, may I help you with your overshoes?" and finished the job without even waiting for a reply.

A keen businessman who saw the boy's deed said to the preacher: "There is a lad who has started life with a success system that simply cannot fail. He is observant. He is thoughtful and helpful. He has the spirit of service and is kindly just like the Master of us all, when he knelt and washed the feet of his disciples in the long ago. In short, the lad is a gentleman. He is more than a Boy Scout doing his one good deed each day; he has the quintessence of greatness in him illustrated in that kind act."

This story is a glorious one in itself, but allow me to call to the attention of my readers the fact that the ability to see in that act something truly great is also important. That is the meaning of this theme for today.

> Give me not scenes more charming, give me eyes
> To see the beauty that around me lies;
> To read the trials of souls, see angels shy
> Among the faces of the passers-by.

We not only get more out of life by doing kindly deeds, but also by having eyes to see them.

"THE MOST BEAUTIFUL SIGHT IN THE WORLD!"

ONCE as I stood on the steps of the Temple of Wisdom in Peking the Chinese who was showing me through the Forbidden City said to me: "What is the most beautiful sight in all the world?"

Naturally I thought he was thinking of beautiful temples, so I named a few: the Taj Mahal in India, the Temple of Borabudur in Java, Notre Dame Cathedral in Paris, St. Peter's in Rome, St. Paul's in London, but he shook his head.

"No, I do not mean temples. They are not the most beautiful sights in the world."

I quickly said: "A glorious sunrise or sunset." I said that because at that time I was writing a book which I later called *A Little Book of Sunsets*.

"No, not sunsets or sunrises."

Then I said: "A beautiful woman—Indian, Chinese, Russian, Japanese—even American."

"No," he smiled, "women are beautiful, but they are not the most beautiful sights in the world."

"Then you mean scenery—the Yangtze Gorge, Mount Taishan, the Grand Canyon, Yellowstone, Mount Everest." I rattled them off.

"No, I do not mean natural scenery. You Americans have the most wonderful natural scenery in all the world, for I have traveled there. I have seen your Niagara Falls, your Grand Canyon, your Arizona afterglow, your Yellowstone, your Mount Shasta, and your Canadian Pacific mountain ranges. Not those!"

"I give up!" I replied with a smile.

"Our philosopher Confucius says: 'The most beautiful sight in the world is a little child going confidently down the road after you have shown him the way.' "

My heart leaped at that statement, for I, at that time had a little child whom I had not seen for months, and that statement appealed to my father-heart. Yes, he was right. That was the most beautiful sight in all the world: a little child going confidently down the road after you have shown him the way.

It is a thought to comfort the hearts of all parents, grand-parents, teachers of little children. Perhaps there is nothing more vital and full of eternal meaning than that act in human life. Perhaps that was what Jesus was thinking and feeling when he said: "Suffer the little children to come unto me, and forbid them not: for of such is the kingdom of God."

SQUIRRELS AND HONEYBEES LIVE TOGETHER

ROGER BABSON, whom I see now and then since he lives near me at Wellesley, Massachusetts, and asks me out to speak to his Sunday evening vesper services, told me of an interesting observation made by his smart daughter.

She used a simple symbol of the world of nature to show him how two diametrically opposed social systems might be able to live together in peace and prosperity. She called his attention to the fact that the honeybee is an out-and-out Communist and the little gray Massachusetts squirrel is an individualist and a capitalist.

"The honeybee," she said to her distinguished father, "thinks nothing of self, puts the fruits of his arduous labor into the common store, and lives successfully a thoroughly collective existence, taking no thoughts for himself or the morrow.

"Your squirrel, on the other hand, is an individualist and a capitalist. He works through the summer months storing up nuts for the winter, thinking nothing of others and always of himself. He hoards acorns all through the fall while they are falling from the oak trees. He buries them in the ground in little lumps, much to the disgust of property owners, and then when winter comes he digs down under the snow to his hoarded securities and eats them. If ever there was a rank individualist, a run-of-the-mill capitalist, that old gray squirrel is certainly one."

"And what is your point, young lady?" asked Mr. Babson. "Why do you call that obvious fact to my attention? What application does it have to life, this strange observation of yours?"

"Did it ever occur to my smart Pop that the squirrel and the bee often live in the same tree in perfect peace, and

111

might it not also be true that we of the human species, even communists and capitalists, might live peaceably together in the same world?"

Roger Babson answered his daughter: "It occurs to me that we shall have to learn to do so if either of us is to survive, my child."

It's a simple parable from everyday life—worth pondering today.

❖❖❖

HOW A REAL KING WORKS

I ONCE sat at the same table with King Prajadhipok of Siam on the old *Santa Cruz* going from Manila to Singapore. He was a young fellow, intensely interested in aviation and baseball, and we had a glorious time talking together.

Landing at Singapore he invited me to come to Siam as his guest for a week or two. As we were saying good-by, being a practical person, I asked him how I should get in touch with him, and he replied nonchalantly: "Oh, just come to the palace!"

He was just returning from Johns Hopkins Hospital, where Dr. Charles Bagley, Jr., had operated on his eyes and saved his sight. Months later Dr. Bagley received a request from the king for a bill, since none had been rendered for the doctor's services.

The request arrived on a day when Dr. Bagley was preparing to go on a much-needed vacation. He was very busy, rather indifferent, as many great surgeons are to the financial part of their work, and he was indifferent even to a bill for his services to a king, just as he was to the services to the poor people. His secretary had a difficult time getting him to notice the request from the king, but she collared him finally with an imperative demand that he pay some attention to the request—for, after all, it was from a king.

The doctor brushed aside the matter by saying: "The king can do no wrong."

The secretary, a young woman with the spirit of adventure and humor, sent the doctor's reply verbatim to the king.

Evidently the young king was kingly both in his character and in his generosity. And it was evident that he decided that his eyesight was worth fifty thousand dollars, for he sent a check for that amount. In any case, it is a good human-interest story, and when I heard the latter part of the story, after hearing the first part about his operation from the king himself, it certainly helped me to reaffirm my faith in human nature.

There is, so it would seem, still something in the figure of speech that has been used for centuries, "He was a kingly person," or, "That was a kingly deed," and, "The king can do no wrong!"

❖❖❖

"SHINGLES AND SUNSETS"

I WAS talking with a group of men sitting on the edge of a swimming pool just after we had had some strenuous exercise. Curiously enough, we got to talking about art.

"What a subject to be discussing on the edge of a swimming pool," said one college professor.

"Ain't art grand?" facetiously quipped a young professor.

"No Harvard professor should say 'ain't,'" was the comment of a Tufts teacher with a good deal of playful sarcasm in his tone.

A Boston University teacher then told us this story. He said that William Hunt, the great artist and teacher, was out on a New England farm sketching with one of his students. The student was painting a landscape which was bathed in the glow and glory of a brilliant sunset—"The glory that the wood receives at sunset in its brazen leaves."

In the foreground, silhouetted against the sunset, was a huge barn. Mr. Hunt watched the young artist for about fifteen minutes as the beautiful colors of the rapidly setting sun were swiftly changing from crimson to gold. His fingers itched to reach for the student's brush and catch the swiftly changing colors in paint.

With no note of criticism Mr. Hunt remarked quietly and impressively to the student: "Son, if you spend too much time on the shingles of that barn you will never have time to paint the sunset, for it is rapidly changing. You'll have to choose between shingles and sunset very soon. What's your choice?"

Startled, the student looked up, then glanced beyond the barn to the glorious sky. His face brightened, his eyes lighted with a great light, he smiled and said: "I choose the sunset, master." I choose the sunset! Who wouldn't when the choice is called to his attention?

In everyday life we have many choices to make, and it all depends upon which choice we make that determines what we really get out of life.

❖❖❖

A HAPPIER WORLD!

A BEAUTIFUL story of kindly service was told to me by the dean of the Boston University School of Music, and it certainly was as interesting to me as it was to those who actually saw the little drama of human interest as it happened on a Boston street one cold winter evening.

The crowds were hurrying toward the Back Bay Station homeward bound. An old man was sitting in front of the Boston Public Library, playing an old battered violin rather crudely. People were pouring out of the popular library, for it was near closing time, but nobody was paying any attention to the old man and his playing.

Suddenly a student of the Boston University School of Music impulsively stopped and looked with pity at the old man, listened for a moment to his untutored playing, then walked over and said: "Please, won't you let me see your violin a minute?"

The man handed it to her with a half doubt in his eyes.

"May I play it, sir?"

That "sir" got him, and he nodded. "Certainly, miss!" he said, and smiled.

She started to play "Ave Maria." It was a gloriously beautiful thing under her deft touch, and the crowds stopped to listen. Soon a score or more people had gathered around that beautiful young girl. She smiled at them and then nodded toward the old man's tin cup as she played. The intention was plain, and the crowd caught the spirit of the music, and coins dropped into the tin cup. A five-dollar bill was stuffed into the already half filled cup by a Back Bay matron.

The man sat weeping with sheer delight and gratitude, and it was because of that story that I went around with the strains of the glorious "Ave Maria" singing in my heart for many days.

It doesn't take much to make this weary old world a sweeter place in which to live, and that young music student sensed that fact and did her bit to make it a happier world for many.

❖❖❖

"SHORTEN YOUR LINE"

HENRY WARD BEECHER was a wise old boy in his day, and his ministry reached far out into life, much farther than mere preaching. Once he gave the world a simple little parable which will appeal to all fishermen and will help even those who never have held a fishing pole in their hands. This is the parable, as he told it:

"When I used to fish in mountain streams, if I had a short line I could direct it more accurately and throw it into this or that pool as I pleased; but if I let out my line until it was twenty or thirty feet long, I could not direct it for I was the victim of every floating stick, jutting rock, and overhanging bough.

"So I have seen men wading down the stream of life, jumping from stone to stone, slipping on this rock and that, and falling into pool after pool because their line was so long that they could do nothing with it—a line that reached down for forty years, or into forty different projects, or in forty different towns. Now if you would avoid those difficulties, friend, shorten your line! Let it reach over one day only. 'Sufficient unto the day is the evil thereof.'"

That parable applies to so many things in life. It applies to the man who tries to do things that his particular talents will not enable him to do. I have always refused to allow anyone to inveigle me into doing something that I knew I was unfitted to do. For instance, I am not a good toastmaster, so I always refuse to be a toastmaster. I do not try to be funny in public speech because I am decidedly not a comedian. I am not an executive by desire, and so I have refused several college presidencies and executive posts. I have learned to shorten my line to those things which I know that I can do and do well.

Many men seem to spread themselves all over creation in business. They expand too rapidly and too far. A man who is perfectly capable of running a small business well, will allow himself to expand until he loses all that he has and fails in the larger enterprise. He has to learn to shorten his line.

116

Other men allow themselves to be roped into so many enterprises outside their own businesses that they fail in their one particular business. That is what Ellis Parker Butler calls "gathering goats' feathers." They allow themselves to become the secretary of this lodge and that; to become the treasurer of the Brick Paving Committee in their local Improvement Association; to head up the Community Chest, the Red Cross drive, and the Blood Donors Advertising Committee. They do all this and neglect their own business through which they make their living. They gather too many "goats' feathers."

Often I have seen a man who had become a great manufacturer or who had amassed a few million dollars turn himself, through the newspapers, into a Jack-of-all-trades. Succeeding in one thing, he felt that he was competent to advise all men on all subjects and he made a fool of himself. "Shorten your line, brother, shorten your line!"

"WE WANT TO SEE GOD"

A MOTHER was putting her little child to bed at night, as we have all done many times, when the child suddenly realized that he was to be left alone in the darkness.

"Mother, am I to be left all alone in the dark?"

"Yes, my dear, but you know you have God with you all the time."

"Yes, I know that God is here with me, but I want somebody who has a face."

The child's desire was, and is, a universal desire. Everyone of us, child and adult, has felt at times that he wanted a God who has a face, who seems real, like a mother or a father, to stay with him in dark hours, whether those dark hours were the dark hours of childhood, when the lights were suddenly turned out in a room, or they were the dark hours of loneliness, death, tragedy, and sorrow. We want something that we can feel and hear and see and touch for our God at such times.

Edwin Markham, with whom I lived intimately for a quarter of a century, gave the most satisfying answer to that universal need when he wrote this little quatrain years ago:

> Here is the truth in a little creed,
> Enough for all the ways we go;
> In Love is all the Law we need;
> In Christ is all the God we know.

Mr. Markham was saying to the human race: "I know that God seems to be a far-off, unattainable being, so far removed from everyday life by theologians and philosophers that he doesn't seem to be real to us in our hours of sorrow and suffering. But Christ is another matter. We do seem to know him, to have seen him; to have gotten close to him in his life on this earth; to have seen him go about healing sickness and lessening the sufferings and loneliness of human beings. We have seen him walk our ways, across our fields, and along our horizons; we have seen him cure people who have suffered with diseases like unto our own; we have seen him die on a cross and rise again. He seems real to us."

That was what Mr. Markham was saying in that simple little quatrain. He was telling us that we can see God in Christ.

The little child was saying the same thing: "Yes, I know that God is here with me, but I want somebody who has a face."

Jesus himself once said: "He that hath seen me hath seen the Father." And he also was answering the world-old desire of humanity to see its God with a face. In fact, that is the real reason that God sent his only-begotten Son to this earth—that humanity might see the face of God in human form.

❖❖❖

"FATHER NEVER FAILED ME!"

SEVERAL years ago I was talking with Dr. Burris A. Jenkins, one of the old war horses of the Christian ministry in Kansas City. He was also a writer of repute, producing several fine books, including novels, and he also edited the *Kansas City Post* for a while. His son Burris, Jr., is a well-known sports cartoonist. Just before he died Dr. Jenkins told me this story:

"When I was a student in college I wronged my father. I secretly became a member of an organization which he had specifically forbidden me to join, in spite of the fact that he was providing for the full expenses of my education and that even the dues which I paid to that organization were a part of his bounty.

"For four years, through all my college course, and for one more year in theological seminary, I kept up the deception. Then came an evening when, as I was preaching to a group of young people in a distant town, I sharply realized my unworthiness to preach to others while my own life cherished that lie.

"I wrote to my father the next morning, confessed what I had done, how for five years I had been deceiving him and accepting his money under a false pretense, told him how sorry I was, and asked his forgiveness, promising to repay every cent to him.

"In answer to my letter I received this telegram: 'It's all right. I forgive you. I knew it two days after you did it. Love. Father.'

"After receiving that loving wire from my father, I could look back through those five years, during which he had offered me the chance to tell him what he already knew. Though I failed him he did not fail me. He patiently waited. He never gave me up. I learned much of faith, love, patience, and forgiveness, such faith and love as God has, from my father. Father never failed me!"

This little silhouette of life is typical of most fathers, and is one of the glorious things about American family life. We do not put much over on our fathers for they have walked the same ways that we walk. Burris Jenkins' father knew of his son's deceit two days after he joined that forbidden fraternity, but he was patient enough to wait until Burris himself acknowledged his wrong and offered to make it right. His father never failed him! My father was that sort of father too. He never failed me. And that's the type of father I want to be.

A BOY BASEBALL DRAMA

IT was the fourteenth straight win of the Boston Red Sox and the whole city was excited about the game. I got on a streetcar headed for Fenway Park. Two boys sat across from me. It was an hour before game time and each boy had a lunch wrapped in paper. They evidently were going into the bleachers and wanted to get there early and had brought their lunches with them. They were as excited at the prospect of eating those lunches as they were about the game.

"My mother put up my lunch. I got two chicken sanwitches and two hot dogs. I got a jelly sanwitch and a peanut butter sanwitch. We could stay in the park a week and not starve. Whatta' you got?"

"I got a lot of sanwitches too, and I gotta big slice of cake my mother made me. No, two slices."

120

"Two slices of cake? Gosh, I wish I had one slice."

"Whatta you think I brought two slices for, nut? One's for you."

I don't know why, but that little drama of two boys sharing the excitement of all Boston over a fourteen-game run of winnings, and that boy who said "Whatta you think I brought two slices for, nut? One's for you!" gave me much to think about. Many times since, as I remember that dialogue of the two baseball pals, I see a new hope for American life. A spirit of sharing! And it is exactly the spirit we have to learn in sharing our bread and meat, our plenty and overflowing abundance, with the starving children of the rest of the world.

"Whatta do you think I brought two slices for, nut? One's for you!"

Atta boy, American small fry! Atta boy! That's the spirit which will win the friendship of the whole world for us. That spirit will bring about a greater victory than our airplanes, battleships, and submarines—and the atomic bomb! The spirit of generosity and sharing will bind the heart of the whole world to this nation with hoops of steel if it becomes general and we are as eager, proud, and willing to share our abundance with those who have little, not even a subsistence diet in most of the world. Less than that spirit will bring us chaos and make us the most despised people of this earth.

❖❖❖

"IF YOU SLOW DOWN EVEN A LITTLE"

BISHOP CANDLER was a great storyteller and one never meets a group of Southern ministers of the Methodist Church these days that he does not hear much about the Candler stories.

The bishop, one story goes, had a certain preacher in his conference who was notoriously lazy. He came to the bishop one day and said to him: "Bishop, I have come to the time of life when I have the feeling that I ought to slow down a little, and therefore I am asking you for a church which does not involve too much work. I've just got to slow down a little."

The old bishop was a realist, and brutally frank when he was dealing with a malingering minister. He snorted in indignation: "Slow down, brother? Slow down? Why, brother, if you slow down even a little, you'll back into somebody behind you!"

About the worst disease that man is heir to in this nation is "the slow-down disease," "the slow-down strike," "the slow-down spirit." These are phrases that I have selected from contemporary American life.

Now that we have won World War II there is a certain self-satisfied lethargy on the spirit of the American people. It is the "slow-down disease" and it is dangerous. In World War I the French had it; they would dig deep trenches, fix them up in comfortable style, dig themselves in, and fight a defensive war. They would lay off for "soup" at ten in the morning, and again at four in the afternoon. They fought a defensive war and prolonged the war many years. With characteristic vigor the Americans went in, put on an active, aggressive campaign of "Let's get it over and go home!" much to the disgust of the French.

It was much the same in World War II. The policy of the armed forces was "the best defense is a good offense." We did not dig in and we did not wait. From island to island we carried an aggressive war in the Pacific until we were at the gates of Japan and Tokyo. That is our American way.

But after the victory over Germany and Japan a seeming

indifference and lethargy came over the American people. We feel that it is all over now, and have thrown overboard the old American army tradition that the best defense is an offense. What we need is to have a Bishop Candler challenge us with a realistic, blunt, brutal slogan directed at our desire to slow down: "Slow down, man? Brother, if you slow down even a little, you'll back into somebody!"

This is no time for the "slow-down disease" in American life if we want to save the world—and our civilization.

❖❖❖

HEARING ONE'S OWN DRUMBEAT

ONE of my favorite haunts is Walden Pond at Concord, Massachusetts. One Fourth of July a small group of us celebrated the one hundredth anniversary of Thoreau's building his little log cabin on the banks of Walden Pond. That celebration sent a lot of us back to Thoreau's books and wise sayings, and that was good for our souls for we read immortal words that fit into the world of this day even more than they did in that great Concord philosopher's day.

For example, this paragraph: "If a man does not keep pace with his companions, do what they do, say what they say, go where they go, do not condemn him. Perhaps it is because he hears a different drummer. Let him step to the music which he hears, however measured or far away that drumbeat may be."

That was Thoreau's plea for the right of a man to follow his own bent, his own vision, his own trumpet call; for that wise man was always saying that every man should be himself. In that respect he was repeating the philosophy of his contemporary Ralph Waldo Emerson, who said in his essay on "Self-Reliance": "Trust thyself! Every heart vibrates to that iron string!"

It is a fine thing for this country, following a global war when so much of our life was regimented, disciplined, and channeled, to go back to the good old American philosophy of individualism, at least in personal development. We have had enough of wartime regimentation. Now we step out of the ranks of the army and become individuals once again. It is only through the development of individual talents, powers, and personalities that we come to our true greatness as persons and as a nation. Nothing worse could happen to our country than that we should mold a race into the same mold and forget individual initiative. That would do away with our Lincolns, our Fords, and our Trumans. That would stifle inventive genius, creative power, and individual leadership. It is a very weak nation which refuses, as Thoreau advises, to allow a man to follow the far-off beat of a drum which he, and he alone, seems to hear.

The very fact that a man refuses to conform is the very hope of that man and of the community, state, or nation to which he belongs. Hitler produced a nation of conformists. The people had no choice; they conformed or died. There was no individual initiative; worse than that, it was disloyalty to have initiative. The result is now a part of the tragic spectacle of history. The land of individual initiative has won the war and stands forth today as the most powerful nation on the earth. It will remain so as long as each individual is permitted and encouraged to listen to his own drumbeat and follow his own genius.

This is still a pioneering nation. It was first of all a nation which pioneered a wilderness; now it is a nation which is pioneering a world. The essence of the pioneer is his individual initiative. That is the soul of progress, invention, and creative art.

❖❖❖

"LIKE CATTLE IN A STORM"

ONE of the faculty members of Boston University School of Theology, Dr. Edwin Prince Booth, lost his son Bray in the paratroop invasion of the Ruhr. I had watched that boy grow up. He had been my caddy on the golf links, and then he had got so good that he could outplay both his father and me. Then we played together.

He went to Harvard and was a sophomore when World War II broke. One day he said to me: "I have been brought up as a preacher's kid, have had everything handed to me on a golden platter. I have never tested my soul. Recently I have been reading a book *Yankee from Olympus,* and it told why Supreme Court Justice Oliver Wendell Holmes, when he was a sophomore in Harvard, left and went into the Civil War when he might have paid a substitute. This is what he said: 'Life is action and passion. It is expected of a man that he share in the action and passion of his time under penalty of being judged not to have lived!' Therefore I want to go into the toughest outfit in the army, the paratroopers."

Into the paratroops he went. His letter came back after his first frightening jump—a letter full of fears, "sweating it out," triumph, and victory. Other letters came from time to time which his father shared with me. Then he came home on a leave, and I took him to lunch. He swaggered as he walked, his hat cocked on the side of his curly blond head, his pants tucked into his paratrooper boots, his cheeks as fair and pink as a girl's, his eyes lighted, a big grin. His walk was a strut, and I loved it in him. Then to the actual front in Europe and his untimely death.

It was a tragedy to all of us. When I heard the news, I went out to comfort his father and mother, my dear friends. However, I felt that I had done and said little, and told Dr.

Booth as much. He replied: "But you are here, Bill! You are here!"

Later in the day Professor McConnell went out on the same errand, and as he was leaving Dr. Booth he said, drawing on an old farmboy memory: "And now, Ted, we'll all have to huddle together like cattle in a storm!" And that to me was the perfect thing to say, the symbol that shared Dr. Booth's grief, the very poetry of sympathy.

❖❖❖

RESEARCH IS A PRAYER

PIERRE CURIE, the great French scientist, who, with his wife, discovered radium in that dramatic moment when he saw a strange, mysterious light glowing in his test tubes, the drama of which was put into a great motion picture, had a reverent sense of the presence of God in all natural phenomena.

One day a student came upon this great French scientist bending low over his microscope. Coming up to him from the rear the student did not see the microscope and thought that he had discovered his professor at prayer. He was about to tiptoe out of the room when the great scientist raised his head and turned.

"Excuse me, sir," stammered the student, "I thought you were praying."

"I was, son," said the professor, returning to his microscope, adding, as he continued watching the miracle on his slide: "All science, research, and study is a prayer; a prayer that God will reveal his eternal secrets to us. For God does have secrets which he reveals only when man searches reverently for them. God did not make all of his revelations in the past. He is continually revealing himself, his plans, and his truths to those who will search for them. Throughout the ages God's revelations are made to man through prophets, scientists, preachers, priests, poets, and musicians. There is beauty in God's universe and he reveals that part of his nature through poets. There is melody, rhythm, and order in his universe and he reveals that to musicians. There is kindness, sacrifice, and love in his universe and he reveals that to little children, great lovers, and kindly and kingly men and women. Yes, my son, I was praying. You were right. Research is always a prayer if it is done reverently."

Aspiration, sacrifice, love, striving, faith, hope, brotherhood; these are all forms of prayer also—prayer which searches, discovers, hopes, and aspires.

❖❖❖

"BUT LOOK HOW HIGH IT IS!"

ONE of my former students, John Homer Miller, wrote a fine book which he called *Take a Look at Yourself,* and in that book he tells a story which Dr. Sylvester Horne used to narrate. It was a story of how that great preacher would tell his classes of the great thoughts that came to him in his garden where he took a daily walk for meditation. He would say to them, quoting from Dorothy Frances Gurney's poem:

> The kiss of the sun for pardon,
>   The song of the birds for mirth;
> One is nearer God's heart in a garden
>   Than anywhere else on earth.

The students were so thrilled with this inspiring thought that they wanted to see the garden where Horne enjoyed his meditations. One day two of his boys came to their professor's house and were invited to go into that sacred garden. They were surprised when they saw nothing but a narrow strip of land surrounded by two high walls.

"Why, Dr. Horne," said one of the boys, "surely this is

not the garden where all your inspiring thoughts come from?

"Oh, yes, it is!" replied the great preacher and teacher.

"But it is so small!"

"Yes, it is small, I admit," replied the teacher, and then pointing to the sky he said: "But look how high it is!"

"I will lift up mine eyes unto the hills" is the way the psalmist-poet says the same thing. It is the upward look which makes life big and high and holy. It is the upward look of reverence, worship, prayer, faith, hope, and vision. It is not important how wide or spacious a garden, a home, or a prayer room is; it is how high it is, how far one may look upward. The upward look is the look toward God, the skies, the clouds, the stars, and an orderly universe.

❖❖❖

"A TWINKLE IN MY EYE"

IN my mother's old scrapbook, which was one of the family heirlooms given to me, and which has been a precious asset to me all my days, I ran across a poem by Margaret Bailey. Here is one verse which says a lot for me and for all of us:

> God, give me sympathy and sense
> And help to keep my courage high.
> God, give me calm and confidence—
> And, please—a twinkle in my eye.

What a glorious, common-sense, workable prayer that is! It is what Professor James used to call "pragmatic"—it works.

I was in Warm Springs, Georgia, once and L. D. Cannon, the manager of the infantile paralysis foundation, told me how he sat behind President Franklin D. Roosevelt on Easter Sunday when he attended his last religious service.

He was a tired, worn-out man. The pressure of life had worn him down. As he sat there Mr. Cannon could see the blood vessels in his forehead and neck throbbing perceptibly, and as he noticed them he looked up and a nurse caught his eyes, and they exchanged significant glances. A few days later when the great president was stricken unto death these two met, and the nurse said: "Do you remember Easter morning when we sat behind the president and both noticed the throbbing in his veins and exchanged glances?

"Yes, I remember."

"We were both thinking the same thing, weren't we?"

"Yes, we were," replied Mr. Cannon.

"He didn't have his old vivacity. He didn't greet us that morning with a spoken word. He was too tired, but he had the old twinkle in his eyes, and he winked at me as he passed out of church. All he had left was a twinkle in his eyes and a wink, but as tired as he was, he used those."

DR. BANTING COULDN'T FORGET JANIE

IN the early twenties, when I was a young pastor in Detroit, Michigan, I heard of two young research workers who were searching for a control of what we then called "sugar diabetes." I went to Toronto, Canada, to interview them. I found them at work in a small laboratory under a stairway. They worked at that problem with little encouragement, a meager financial background, and yet with a scientific devotion and sacrifice. Then in 1922 they discovered insulin, one of the most beneficent revelations of God that had come up to that time, an absolute control of sugar in the blood, a discovery which would give diabetics new hope of living a fairly normal and happy life through its use.

In the years which have intervened since that time insulin has been an accepted benefit to countless millions of afflicted human beings.

Not until a year ago, when I read *Banting's Miracle,* did I learn of the motive that was back of Dr. Frederick G. Banting's research. It seems that when he was a country boy he knew a little girl named Janie. He loved her because she could climb trees, play ball, hockey, skate, and hunt as well as a boy. Then one day he heard his parents say that Janie was seriously ill. A few days later he heard them say that she was in a "coma," a word he didn't even understand. Then she died. Young Banting was one of the boy pall-pearers who carried her little body to a Canadian hillside God's acre for burial.

Years passed and Dr. Banting seriously considered going into the ministry but rejected that. Later he seriously considered being a missionary (always seeking the service motive) but rejected that. Then finally he decided to go into research work. The author of his life makes this simple statement as to why he finally choose research work: "It was because the memory of what had happened to his little Janie haunted him day and night and would not let him rest. So he devoted his time and talents to discovering a control of "sugar in the blood" so that no other little Janies would die an untimely death in the very morning of life." Dr. Banting couldn't forget Janie and what happened to her.

❖❖❖

A GLORIOUS ADVENTURE IN STEWARDSHIP

ON a trip into North Carolina I heard of an old man and his wife, both in their seventies, who were doing a unique thing in giving. His name is Harvey Wood Murdock. I asked for an interview and was driven by car from Statesville to see him. We drove up to a tumble-down old farmhouse, unpainted and crude. There were several outbuildings, all unpainted and unimproved. The old man had on rather crude jeans and a blue shirt. There were no modern improvements in that home; they got their water from an old well like the immortal well of "The Old Oaken Bucket"; they had outdoor toilet facilities; they had never owned an automobile; they lived simply, almost meagerly.

Yet that old man and woman were wealthy beyond imagination. They owned a thousand acres of land in Oklahoma, on which there were gas and oil wells which brought them in an annual income which gave them the right to live in luxury. I had already been told by my guides of the great sums they were giving annually to good works in North Carolina. As we sat there I determined on a very dramatic and personal question and said: "Mr. Murdock, you have immense wealth, and yet you live here in this old house without any modern improvements—no steam heat, no running water, toilet facilities outside. Why don't you use some of your wealth for personal comfort in your old age?"

He turned to me as naïvely as a child, not at all offended by my personal question, smiled, and said: "That's funny, but my wife and I were talking about that very thing last night as we sat on this porch listening to our mockingbirds singing. And we decided that we would do that very thing just as soon as we have paid that $25,000 to the Children's Home, that $5,000 to the new college, that $10,000 to the Crusade for Christ."

My heart was subdued, my feelings were deeply touched at this simple, dignified answer to my question. A cardinal flashed in the sunlight and came to rest in a nest in honeysuckle vines which covered an old-fashioned well. The air

131

was beautiful with color and sweet with the scent of honey-suckle—and something else which could not be put into mere words.

✤✤✤

THE SECRET OF LONG LIFE AND HAPPINESS

A REPORTER, as is usually the case when a man reaches the ripe old age of one hundred or more, was assigned to interview a certain old character in the Southland when he arrived at his 104th birthday.

When the reporter arrived the old man was awaiting him at the gate of his farm with eagerness and anticipation, all dressed up in his Sunday best, for that interview was an event to him.

The first question the reporter asked this smiling, happy-looking old man was the usual one on such occasion: "Just what is the secret of your long and happy life, Mr. Jones?"

"Well," replied that simple old man, with a smile, "every morning when I get out of bed (and I want you to know that I do get out of bed around daylight when the mockingbirds begin to sing) I go over to the window. Then I say to myself when I look out, whether it is raining, snowing, or sunny: 'This is exactly the kind of a day I wanted!'"

"But that sounds like a sort of a Pollyanna philosophy, Mr. Jones," said the young and facetious reporter.

"I don't know who this Pollyanna is; I never heard her name in this neighborhood, and I know everybody here. But no matter what this Pollyanna you mention says or thinks, that's my story and I stick to it. And what is more, son, my philosophy works. And ain't I here after a hundred and four years? Ain't I here, Son?"

When I heard that wise tale I remembered a short verse

which I recently taught to my grandsons, much to their delight:

> If you want to be happy,
> I'll tell you the way;
> Don't live tomorrow
> Until you've lived today.

And like 104-year-old Mr. Jones, take the days as they come, rain or sunshine, wind or calm, warm or cold, and say: "This is exactly the kind of a day I wanted!" Take it as it comes and don't fret your soul, for you can't do anything about it anyhow.

❖❖❖

A PRAYER FOR COURAGE

A CERTAIN magazine for which I write asked me to write a series of twenty-five prayer poems which they wanted to run as a special feature in a box on their editorial page. I accepted this assignment and waited for the muse to give me the prayer poems.

One day I visited a hospital for wounded and handicapped soldiers near Boston. There I saw men who had been blinded in the war, legless men dancing and having a hilarious time with their nurses at an evening social event, men who had no arms, men who were eating their meals with hooks and artificial hands and fingers.

And what impressed me so deeply was that I did not see a single long countenance among all those two thousand boys. They laughed, danced, sang, shouted, whistled, and made merry in a glorious way.

One of the nurses said to me, when I made a comment about their hilarity, with the implication that it might be just put on as an act because I was a visitor: "No! They're always that way. In fact, I come to work every day with little songs singing in my heart over my anticipation of a happy day with my boys. No matter what the weather is, no matter how gloomy my outside invironment has been the night before (and it is always darker and more pessimistic than it is in this hospital) I always know that these boys will cheer my heart before the day is over. They have the very essence of courage in their souls."

And right then and there I had one of my prayer poems, and here it is:

> God of the oak and jutting rocks,
>   God of the rugged granite peak,
> Amid life's blasts and bitter shocks
>   We come to Thee, this day, to seek
> Thy strength, Thy courage, and repose;
>   Thy faith, Thy hope, Thy certainty,
> To face whatever ills and woes
>   May come within our destiny.

❖❖❖

"I SAW GOD WASH THE WORLD"

I HAVE received more than ten thousand letters in the last thirty years asking me the story which inspired the writing of "I Saw God Wash the World." Here is that story told in print for the first time, and I use it to celebrate a new edition of my little book of poems by that title.

It was in 1917, in San Jose, California. It had rained all night in a deluge which must have been like Noah's little rain. Californians call it "a slight dew" or "a heavy fog."

But when morning broke there was a glorious white sunlight which turned the world to silver. I looked out of our sleeping porch. There was an old pepper tree in the back yard with long slender green leaves. It looked as if God had

134

washed every green leaf and every cluster of red berries on that tree. To the right of our back yard I had planted a garden of white roses, and to the left a garden of huge cabbagelike red roses. It looked as if every red and white rose had had its face washed in the night. A green hummingbird was poised over a honeysuckle bush, and it also looked as if God had washed its green wings until they literally shone in the morning light with a glorious, almost dazzling, brilliance. I said to Mrs. Stidger: "It looks as if God had washed the world last night."

That phrase sang in my soul through dressing, shaving, and breakfast. When I climbed into my automobile, an open car, the rhythmic beat of the engine and the whir of the wheels sang, "I saw God wash the world last night, I saw God wash the world last night, I saw God wash the world last night." That phrase sang in my soul all the way to my study at First Church, and I immediately sat down and wrote the poem. It was first published in the old *Epworth Herald,* and then was copied all over the world, translated into more than twenty languages. It found its way into anthologies, including Bartlett's *Familiar Quotations.* And that is the simple story of how "I Saw God Wash the World" came into being.

❖❖❖

"AH, WOULD HE HAD WASHED ME"

I FOLLOW up the preceding story of the writing of "I Saw God Wash the World" with the reason why I think this poem appeals to so many people. It is because the last verse has in it the implications of redemption, conversion, rebirth, and the changed life—the thing which happened to Jesus on the River Jordan, and the thing which happened to Paul on the road to Damascus. That is a universal hunger of the human soul, expressed in the psalm: "Purge me with hyssop, and I shall be clean: wash me, and I shall be whiter than snow."

Several years after writing the poem I changed the last line in it, and that is the only change which has been made. Instead of using the figure of "that old pepper tree," which I first used, I changed it to "that old white birch tree" for two reasons. First, the pepper tree is a tropical tree and is not as universally known as a white birch tree. Second, the image of a white birch tree is one of immaculate cleanness in itself, and says exactly what I was trying to say. It is a great preaching idea which reoccurs frequently in both the Old and the New Testament—the idea of the cleansed soul, the new start, the washed spirit. The last four lines are the heart of the preaching possibilities and the spiritual meaning of this poem:

> I saw God wash the world last night.
> Ah, would He had washed me
> As clean of all my dust and dirt
> As that old white birch tree.

The Bible frequently reiterates that theme: "May I not wash in them, and be clean?" (II Kings 5:12.) "I will wash mine hands in innocency." (Ps. 26:6.) "Wash me thoroughly from mine iniquity." (Ps. 51:2.) "Wash me, and I shall be whiter than snow." (Ps. 51:7.) "Wash you, make you clean!" (Isa. 1:16.) "Wash thine heart!" (Jer. 4:14.) "Go, wash in the pool of Siloam!" (John 9:7.) "That . . . washed us from our sins." (Rev. 1:5.) "They . . . have washed their robes." (Rev. 7:14.)

❖❖❖

"THAT I REGRET!"

IN Statesville, North Carolina, lives a young Methodist minister, Dr. Charles Bowles, and he has two sons, Charles and Joe. Those two sons, like all youngsters, have their brief moments of belligerency, quarreling, and antagonism.

One morning they were at it hammer and tongs, and young Joe came to his father complaining that Charles had kicked him on the shins, and in other diverse ways had subjected his body to certain indignities and roughness.

"I hate that guy!" Joe said to his father, who listened patiently to his complaints.

"Yes, but after all, Joe, Charles is your brother" said this parson-father, gently, expecting that profound statement to dissipate all of his younger son's indignation.

Young Joe paused a moment in deep thought, and his father felt that his little preachment had gone home. Then Joe looked up and said: "That I regret, Dad!"

Dr. Bowles was a little disappointed that his homily hadn't seemed to convert Joe, and he sat in meditation, thinking how that little domestic drama was the heart of the world's problems and the world's hope also: racial predjudice; the hatred of Jews, Negroes, Japanese, Germans; black against white; Russian against the world; yet all brothers in the world-family. If they could only remember that they were brothers. But no, the brothers of the world seemed to be saying, "That I regret!" to the Master who once said, "Our Father which art in heaven," with that prayer's implication of a world family.

While Dr. Bowles was still chagrined that Joe didn't seem to catch the implications of brotherhood, he looked up and saw Joe with his arms around Charles, hugging him with brotherly affection and forgiveness. And as he did so, he grinned and said to his father in explanation of his sudden

137

reversal of feeling: "After all, Dad, Charles is my brother, isn't he?"

❖❖❖

"AND THERE'S SOMETHING IN THE AIR"

ONE day I was invited to visit Mr. Henry Ford at Dearborn when John Burroughs, his naturalist friend, was also there. We had a luncheon at the now-famous round table and walked in the woods all afternoon while Mr. Burroughs and Mr. Ford watched the birds through their bird glasses. Mr. Ford showed Mr. Burroughs how he had ingeniously hung baltimore oriole nests on piano wire because the birds liked to have their nests swaying in the winds. Mr. Burroughs was fascinated with that ingeniousness, and that the orioles had actually accepted Mr. Ford's device for hanging their nests.

That evening we sat in Mr. Ford's office, which looked out on a beautiful artificial lake, and I asked Mr. Burroughs what had inspired him to write his beautiful poem which he called "Waiting." He replied: "Just such an evening as this. A glorious golden sunset was dying out on the northern New York hills at 'Slabsides.' I sat on my chair on the porch, and that poem came. If I have any immortality or lasting fame, it will come to me through that poem."

Our hearts were hushed and calm as we sat there looking out on Mr. Ford's lake. A Michigan Central train thundered by, and was gone in a moment, only to leave behind it even an accentuated peace and quiet, and not a word was spoken for five minutes. That sense of peace was still on my soul when I got home, and I wrote this poem:

There's a glory on the water,
And a splendor in the sky,
When the day has come to sunset
And the night-winds sing and sigh.

There's a golden pathway gleaming
   And the clouds are touched with light;
Where the sun, in love, is leaning
   On the bosom of the night.

There's a leap of love and longing,
   And there's something in the air,
When the day has come to sunset,
   Which is close akin to prayer.

❖❖❖

A QUARREL WITH A WAITER

I WALKED nonchalantly into a dining car one day for lunch. It was already one-thirty, and naturally I thought that lunch was set up.

I seated myself and a burly Negro waiter came, like a huge elephant on charge, and yelled at me: "Lunch ain't set up yet! What you don' here? Lunch ain't set up yet! We'll call when it's ready!" He was what you would mildly term as "nasty."

Rising from my chair I turned on that waiter and said, as calmly as I could: "I didn't know that lunch was not set up, and I'll wait until it is called, but why couldn't you be a gentleman and a Christian in addressing me? After all, you are just employed here. You are supposed to be the servant of the patrons and not a top sergeant. Why don't you learn to be nice about it?"

I walked out, waited for the call to lunch to be officially made, went back into the dining car. The steward met me with an apology: "I'm sorry that boy talked to you that way, but I'm glad that you called him for it. I've been trying to train these waiters to be courteous, but it doesn't always take."

"Just seat me at his table and I'll make up to him for

139

being abrupt," I requested. But I didn't need to make up anything. He did all the making up. He bowed to me; he watched my every need; he hovered over me; he jumped at my mild requests. He "sir'd" me, he literally patted me on my bald head with his gentleness and his service. It was just what he needed and what a lot of public servants need to hear from the public when they are impolite.

I half-apologized to him before the meal was over, ending by repeating my original phrase: "Why can't you be nice like a Christian gentleman?" At that he replied to me: "And dat's jes it, sir, I is a Christian and I certainly didn't ack lak one. I'ze plumb ashamed of myself. I is a Christian and I didn't ack like one!"

Needless to say the waiter received double the tip he would have received and he learned a lesson he will not forget. I not only appreciated that experience but the steward did also, and I know that the waiter did for he chuckled as I arose.

❖❖❖

"PUT 'ER THERE, COMRADE!"

WHEN the late Cyrus Dallin, the great American sculptor, was living I had the privilege of knowing him intimately, and what is more important, the privilege of knowing his great works from the Atlantic to the Pacific: "The Appeal to the Great Spirit" in Boston, "Samoset" in Plymouth, "The Pioneer Mother," in front of the State House in Boston, "The Medicine Man" in Philadelphia, "The Signal of Peace" in Chicago, "The Scout" in Kansas City, and many others. One day I asked him where I could see what he looked upon as his greatest work—"The Spirit of Life." He told me that it was on a great estate in Brookline and that if I wanted to see it I was just to drive into that estate and make myself at home. If anybody attempted to

140

stop me, I was just to tell them that the sculptor himself had sent me to see that beautiful work.

I took him at his word, and one day, nonchallantly, almost brazenly, drove into that private estate, until I found "The Spirit of Life" standing beside a fountain and a pool. It was a mother holding a baby aloft in her hands above her head; a beautiful piece of bronze as it was reflected in the placid water of the pool, the pool itself fringed with beautiful rosebushes.

As I was standing there, lost in the beauty of that immortal bronze, a guard suddenly charged across the lawn, yelling as he came with a belligerent yelp in his brawny voice: "What are you doing on this estate?"

I was a bit upset by his bull-like charge and said: "You might have guessed, my friend. I am looking at this beautiful bronze which my friend Cyrus Dallin did, and—with his permission."

"Did you get permission from Mr. L—— who owns this estate?" he asked in the same belligerent tone.

"No, I'm afraid I didn't take that precaution," I replied just as belligerently as he.

"Then you'll have to beat it. No visitors are permitted on this estate without a special written permit."

At that I turned on him, more facetiously than seriously, thinking I would try a subtlety on him, and said: "Listen here, my friend, when the revolution comes we'll just break up these big estates and let the people have a chance to see these universal works of art."

His face lighted up at that statement, a smile came over his otherwise surly countenance, and he replied, reaching out his hand: "Put 'er there, comrade. I'm with you for the revolution!"

❖❖❖

"REALISM DOWN TO EARTH"

BISHOP BRUCE BAXTER used to tell the story of a man who had a precocious son who wanted a horse for Christmas more than he wanted anything else. The father tried to talk him out of it, telling him that they couldn't keep a horse in the city.

"But I want a horse, and I don't want anything but a horse!" whined the three-year-old.

Endeavors to compromise with the child for the much desired horse, the father found, were of no avail. He got a picture of a horse in colors and brought that home. The little fellow said: "That isn't a real horse, daddy!"

And when his father brought home a cardboard horse, as large as the boy himself, once again he heard: "But that isn't a real horse, daddy. I want a real horse!" There was a plaintive note in his voice.

The father bought a book showing pictures of horses, every type of horse from a pony to a race horse, beautiful steeds, Kentucky thoroughbreds, with jockeys on them, horses out in the pasture, and sleek steeds in races. But the boy was adamant: "I want a horse that's made out of horse!"

The little boy did not want a substitute for a "horse that's made out of horse." He wanted realism.

In these hectic days everyone seems to offer substitutes; there is a lack of realism in preaching, politics, and other fields. A generation ago Carl Sandburg wrote a poem entitled "To a Contemporary Bunkshooter," which was directed at Billy Sunday. If Sandburg wrote his poem today he could dedicate it to many people. As we listen to these "bunkshooters" we control our almost irresistible urge to annihilate them. These tear-jerkers, calamity howlers, disaster exaggerators are always in a dither, in a state of great excitement about nothing much.

In our everyday American way of living we need "a horse that's made out of horse." We want honest-to-goodness realism in our writing, thinking, and feeling. We're weary of the "bunkshooters."

❖❖❖

"DOWN DEEP UNDER—A MEMORY"

ONE of our student chaplains told me this one:

One Sunday night the chapel of a large air base in Italy was crowded when suddenly an intoxicated corporal staggered in and lunged his way toward the altar bawling out a comic song at the top of his lungs.

"Pipe down!" yelled a dozen indigant voices.

"Toss the dumb guy out on his neck!" yelled others.

"Leave him alone, men," said the chaplain, "let's just see what he will do."

The corporal staggered up to the platform yelling: "I can sing as well as any of you—and preach too, Gov'nor," and looking through bleary eyes at the Chaplain, standing patiently by.

"Let's see what you can do," answered the chaplain, much to the surprise of the indignant men.

With a silly grin the poor fellow weaved to the platform, turned to the chaplain, and leered, as he said with great bravado: "Now, chaplain, what shall it be—a song, a sermon, or a prayer?"

"You'd better pray, Son," said the chaplain.

The soldier seemed to sober for an instant, and then shut his eyes. "Let us pray!" said the chaplain reverently.

Controlling his speech with difficulty the drunken man started: "O God . . ." A long pause, then: "O God . . ."

Then came a sob which literally tore through every heart present. The boy's head sank. He turned to the chaplain, whose arms were around him in an instant: "I had a good mother, sir. Once she taught me . . ." He choked up and could go no further.

Then the chaplain prayed earnestly for that boy, his mother, and for every man there, and thanked God for all Christian homes.

ACKNOWLEDGMENTS

ACKNOWLEDGMENT is made to the following copyright owners for their gracious permission to reproduce in this volume the selections noted:

BURNS, OATS, & WASHBOURNE, LTD. for lines from "The Lord God Planted a Garden" by Dorothy Frances Gurney.

HARPER'S MAGAZINE for lines from "April Rain" by Robert Loveman.

THE MACMILLAN COMPANY for lines from *The Everlasting Mercy* by John Masefield.

VIRGIL MARKHAM for selections from poems by his father, Edwin Markham. Used by special permission.

THE STRATFORD COMPANY for lines from "Grace Before Work" by Margaret Bailey.

INDEX OF TITLES

148

INDEX OF PERSONS

151

Powell, Marie Cole, 18
Prajadhipok, King, 112

Quiz Kids, 20

Roosevelt, Franklin D., 128
Roosevelt, Quentin, 102
Roosevelt, Theodore, 102
Ruopp, Harold, 72

Sandburg, Carl, 142
Santayana, George, 58
Schwab, Charles M., 85
Scott, Mary, 18
Shakespeare, 20
Stanton, Edwin, 58
Steinmetz, Charles, 59
Stevenson, Robert Louis, 53, 107
Stout, William, 56

Sun Yat-sen, 32
Sunday, William (Billy), 142

Thoreau, Henry D., 50, 123
Tolstoy, 103
Tuttle, Mrs. Lee, 34

Van Dyke, Henry, 67

Walcot, William, 101
Wells, H. G., 48
Wesley, John, 107
Whitehead, Alfred North, 13
Wilkins, Saunders, 18
Willkie, Wendell, 34
Wilson, Dorothy Clarke, 87
Woollcott, Alexander, 94
Wright, Orville, 56
Wright, Richard, 103

INDEX OF TOPICS

153

Penitence, 12
Poetry
  Anonymous
    "And always when the old
      year ends," 40
    "Friendship is like a gar-
      den," 39
    "Give me not scenes more
      charming, give me eyes,"
      108
    "If you want to be happy,"
      133
  Bailey, Margaret
    "God, give me sympathy
      and sense," 128
  Browning, Robert
    "Grow old along with me,"
      38
    "That's the wise thrush; he
      sings each song twice
      over," 63
    "The common problem,
      yours, mine, everyone's,"
      100
  de Louk, Louis
    "A baby smiled in its moth-
      er's face," 31
  Gurney, Dorothy Frances
    "The kiss of the sun for
      pardon," 127
  Hartwich, Ethelyn Miller
    "Great roads the Romans
      built that men might
      meet," 54
  Landor, Walter Savage
    "I strove with none, for
      none was worth my
      strife," 64
  Loveman, Robert
    "It is not raining rain to
      me," 94
  Markham, Edwin
    "Here is the truth in a
      little creed," 118
    "The robber is robbed of
      his riches," 87

  Masefield, John
    "His eyes forever on some
      sign," 52
    "Oh, mother, when I think
      of thee," 45
  Shakespeare
    "To you your father should
      be a god," 20
  Stidger, William L.
    "God of the oak and jutting
      rock," 134
    "I saw God wash the world
      last night," 136
    "There's a glory on the
      water," 138
    "There's a golden pathway
      gleaming," 139
Prayer, 126-27, 133, 143
Pride, 21

Rehabilitation, 53, 78
Religion, 143-44
Repartee, 11
Roads, 53-54

Sacrifice, 26-27, 30, 44-45
Self-reliance, 34-35, 123
Service, 12-13, 18, 30, 70
Sharing, 30, 82-83
Smiles, 31
Sorrow, 11-12
Spirit, 23-24
Stars, 57-58
Storms, 12, 125-26
Struggle, 15
Suffering, 11-12
Sympathy, 71-73, 106-7

Teachers, 17-18
Tears, 11-12
Tenderness, 12-13
Transformation, 17-18

Visions, 14-15, 33-34, 123-24

Youth, 11-13, 15-17, 19-20, 24-25

154